WOOD PELLET AND SMOKER GRILL COOKBOOK

The ultimate GUIDE TO GRILLING for beginners, and the most complete barbecue recipes book

TABLE OF CONTENTS

INTRODUCTION

Barbecue is an extremely old culinary art from the Stone Age when Neanderthals roasted meat over open fires. It didn't even have a name back then; it was just a way of life. If Neanderthals couldn't find any food, they ate each other. It is believed that Neanderthal is still a delicacy today in China. As human civilization progressed, the art of barbecue gradually advanced from the stone age to the iron age, the bronze age, the new age, until finally arriving at its final destination: the computer age.

Today, the art of barbecue is more technologically advanced than ever. Barbecue is no longer just a mechanical way of cooking and eating food but a well-recognized fine culinary art in its own right. It even has a special culinary society just for the fine art of barbecue, and a series of educational cookbooks and other media to expand knowledge of the subject.

Barbecuing was refined by the Native Americans who called it "suck it, pull it, and wipe it." It wasn't until 1645 that the English settlers brought barbecue to the United States and called it "Hamburg Style." Today it's called "Pork and Beans." During the Civil War, the south was famous for its barbecuing, barbecue spareribs was the most popular dish.

1

The North's contribution was "Sauerkraut and Weenie Roast." The north won the war; however, they still have not found a cure for "Weenie Roast."

The barbecue war ended with "Smoked Plank." The south was flooded with loaded white-creamed potatoes. The north was devastated by home-made Heinz barbecue sauce. The north surrendered in 1865 and the south in 1869. An armistice was called "Burgoo." Barbecue was banned after the Civil War. At the end of the War, the south could not take the North's dry, weird tasting meat anymore. The south hid in the woods and ate poisonous things like fern beans, Dinah-jellybean, and morinda. So, to make up for it, the south invented the "Pig Pickin' yinzer."

Barbecue was banned again during WW2. The south made a barbecue chicken called "Barbecue Romano." The north made a barbecue steak called "Hamburger Steak." Both kinds of meat tasted the same, with the taste of "Practice making icing." It was called the "Jeepney Massacre." Barbecue was reintroduced after the war, it was called "Red, Hot & Grill." The barbecue war started when it was introduced in the 1950s. It was called: "Crackling Rosy Barbecue." The war was over when President Reagan said "let's throw another chopper on it."

Barbecue has changed a lot since its inception. Today, you can even buy it already cooked; chefs cook it in joints, shacks, honkies, shanties, and cabins. They can cook it because of the invention of the smoker. BBQ is very popular across the world. It is Mexican, American, Asian, European, African, and Scandinavian barbecue. The barbecue was invented by Native Americans, Europeans, Africans, and Scandinavian people.

THE SMOKING EQUIPMENT

S moking equipment and grills come in many shapes, sizes, and price ranges. Which 1 you'll on what you plan to use it for, how often you plan to use it, and what you can afford. If you and your family like lots of activities or cooking outdoors, it makes sense to invest in a good quality smoker and grill. And if you live in a part of the world where weather permits outdoor cooking and living for most of the year (e.g., South Africa or Australia), buying 1 of these devices makes even more sense.

A good-quality wood pellet smoker and grill can last for decades, so choosing 1 that is expensive but reliable is considered a good investment. Besides, most profitable brands come with a 3-year warranty, which guarantees they are made of high-quality materials and are made to last. If you enjoy outdoor cooking, investing in a high-quality smoker and grill should not be a dilemma; however, if you barbecue only once or twice a year, for Christmas and a birthday, you shouldn't bother buying the top of the range stuff. Therefore, your lifestyle and your plans with the grill will decide which 1 you should buy.

Most people who enjoy grilled food love the smell and flavor of smoke. However, the amount of smoke that a pellet can produce depends on the temperature and the type of shell used. At first, the shots create a lot of smoke, but once the ignition stage is over and pellets start settling towards target temperature, a steadier light-colored smoke will appear. Sometimes, it may not even be visible.

When you use high-quality pellets, you will get the maximum amount of smoke as well as flavor. However, remember that not all shells create an equal amount of smoke. The amount of smoke depends on the density of the wood. The apple doesn't smoke as well as hickory or oak. Besides, if you don't clean your fire pot and it's full of ash, the smoke quantity will be cheaper than it would have done, including the clean facilities.

Smoking Techniques

The essential ingredient of all food-smoking techniques is vapor. Smoke is generated through flaming, which is what happens when oxygen is exposed to fuel, which may come essentially as a shock to many, but smoke has flavor and color. Depending on the heat source, e.g., wood, coal, gas, wood pellets, etc., smoke can smell refreshing, energizing, and fragrant as well as disgusting and appalling. It how you create different flavors of the food you smoke by varying natural heat sources.

2 Primary Ways of Smoking Food:

1. **Hot smoking:** this reminds us of smoked food. With this method, food is exposed to heat and smoke for several minutes to several hours. The smoke and the heat "cook" the food. To enhance the flavor and accelerate drying, some foods are cold-smoked first before they are exposed to hot smoke.

2. **Cold smoking:** this is when food is smoked at about 85° F without being exposed to heat. This process can take 3 weeks, and the result is drier, saltier food. Although considered a delicacy, foods smoked this way is still considered "raw" after smoking and should be cooked either before or after cold-smoking.

Food is smoked this way because, during the cold smoking process, food develops a unique flavor. However, this method also requires careful monitoring, so the food does not develop harmful bacteria. Right conditions for cold drying are not easy to achieve in warm environments, so this method is practiced mainly in the cold northern regions, e.g., Scandinavia, Siberia, etc.

During the cold smoking process, the smoke is not produced in the chamber where the food is but in the neighboring compartment. Once enough smoke is created, it is directed to where the food is through pipes to cool before reaching the food. So, food is exposed to cold smoke, and it dries very slowly because of the lack of heat.

Ideally, food should be preserved this way only in dry and cold environments. The advantage of cold smoking over hot smoking is that food exposed to cold smoke has a unique flavor, and the cold smoke adds phenols and other chemicals that have an antimicrobial effect on the food. On the other hand, hot smoking is less efficient with preserving food from bacteria and is primarily used to improve the taste and impart wood flavor to the food.

Essential Gear

Grilling gear and accessories abound. If you have these tools at the ready, you'll be good to grill and make any of the recipes in this book.

- **Basting brush:** a basting meeting is invaluable for applying sauces to meat on the grill. Look for an encounter with a long handle and sturdy, heat-resistant bristles, such as silicone.

- **Digital instant-read thermometer:** this is a handheld thermometer with a probe and digital readout that quickly tells you whether your food is cooked to its proper doneness.

- **Disposable foil pans:** aluminum foil pans are convenient for transferring food from the grill to the kitchen or eating destination. Also, they are great drip pan stand-ins.

- **Grill brush:** a coil brush is ideal for cleaning cooking grates of food debris and residue before cooking. Avoid wire brushes; stray wires can stick to the grill after cleaning and wind up in your food.

- **Grilling basket or topper:** this perforated metal basket holds vegetables or smaller foods that may slip through the cooking grate.

- **Metal spatula:** you'll need a spatula for food like burgers or fish that might break apart while flipping and turning. Look for a wider spatula with a long handle designed explicitly for grilling.

- **Mitts:** heat-resistant mitts protect your hands from burns when you need to handle hot grill lids, cooking grates, and even platters of hot food. Choose gloves with fingers for maximum functionality and range of motion. I recommend fleece-lined welding gloves if you're looking to upgrade.

- **Skewers:** skewers hold meat or veggies together while cooking and can maximize your grilling space. Stainless steel is preferred over wood that can burn over high heat.

- **Surface thermometer:** this thermometer is placed on your cooking grates and measures the temperature of the surface your food is cooking on. Choose 1 that registers to a minimum of 600° F and is made specifically for grills.

Tongs: you'll use these frequently to turn food while it's cooking and to take food on and off the grill safely. Choose spring-loaded tongs that are at least 12 inches long to protect your hands. Avoid plastic tips that could melt under high heat. Grilling forks should be avoided, as they pierce cooked proteins, which results in the loss of essential moisture from the food.

THE WOOD PELLET GRID

Pellet grills combine the best components of smokers, gas/charcoal barbecues, and furnaces to give you the best results. They are the best outdoor cookers, and with the help of natural hardwood pellets, they offer both direct and incidental heat. Generally, wood pellets are used as the primary fuel source. These pellets are drained into a storage container called a tank; the shells are slowly fed into the cooking chamber nestled within. The grill has an auger that helps to complete this process. Powered by electricity, flaming helps to light the wood pellets, ultimately heating the cooking room thoroughly. The design includes fans because air is a natural and essential part of the cooking process, this air helps to disperse the heat and smoke regularly through the cooking area.

1 of the essential benefits of grilling with these pellets is that these grills offer precise temperature settings. The temperature can be set using a dial or through a digital keypad. Thanks to technology, these grills come with fancy locations that offer several cooking options, direct/indirect heat, and heat probes that ensure that the meat cooks right through and at the desired temperature.

The wood pellets are essential and unique to such grills. Generally, these pellets are made from all-natural hardwood. Such high-quality hardwood is dried and then ground into sawdust. Later, compact wood pellets are created out of sawdust that is pressurized at high and extreme temperatures. The process is tight and is designed to be the most comfortable fuel for home use. It means that it produces less than 1 percent of ash. This is great because it makes after-cooking clean-up a breeze.

The other advantage is that these wood chips add a punch of flavor without a lot of effort on your side. Further, the grill's fans ensure that the meat is continuously cooked and evenly throughout. An additional bonus with the wood pellet smoker-grill is that you can cook without having to babysit the meat or food. Cooking slow and long is now possible, and comfortable too. For instance, many consider cooking a brisket to be complicated and cumbersome.

However, with a wood pellet smoker-grill, it is fuss-free, the only work you must put in is to ensure that your storehouse (chamber for fuel) is always packed with pellets, ensuring no fuel shortage. There are some of the other benefits that make this the perfect way to cook: 1 of the biggest problems most people have with cooking on a grill is the frequent flare-ups.

Imagine stepping into your kitchen to grab something. You return to find flames shooting up from your grill. You can easily avoid such an experience with the wood-pellet grill, as the firepot is well protected from direct contact with the food. It features a heat deflector and a grease drip tray, too. Further, the fan helps to keep the air well-circulated and entirely in control.

Have you ever thought about cooking grilled chicken but eventually gave up because your hunger pangs would not survive the time it would take to heat the grill and then cook the chicken to perfection? The wood pellet smoker-grill offers the perfect solution short on time (which is pretty much everyone these days!). Hereabouts, all you need to do is pick the temperature and allow the grill to do the rest for you. So, let's look at the history of how this kind of cooking procedure evolved.

History of the Wood Pellet

The smoking of food goes way back to the Paleolithic ages, as simple dwellings lacked chimneys through which the smoke could escape. In such places, the meat would develop a unique and distinctive flavor. Having recognized this, early humans combined this process with curing meats by using salt or brine. It was found to be an effective food preservation method. Arts around the world had some way resembling the same to preserve and flavor their meat.

Therefore, smoking the meat was more of a preservation method than a form of spicing it. However, with time, transportation methods improved, and it shifted easier to move food. Smoking began to be used to add flavor rather than to preserve food.

The smoking process is simple, as it is based on the thought of cooking food over smoke. If you go back in time, you will see that the term "Smoke House" was used about farmhouses. Farms featured a miniature building where meats could be vaporized and stored. This building was not attached to the main house due to risks of fire, smoke emanations, and the possibility that smoking could introduce certain hydrocarbons into the food.

Gradually, as more people began to smoke and store meat, it became more innovative. A large-scale prototype of a commercial smokehouse was first produced in 1939. Created in Scotland, this kiln allowed for uniform smoking in large quantities. It was the original version, though time and technology have given us far better and more compact representations.

Cultures around the world use different fuels to add flavor to their cooking. For instance, in Europe, alder seems to be the popular smoking timber, but oak and beech are often used. You can find many options (such as pecan, hickory, oak, and mesquite, and fruit trees such as plum, apple, and cherry) used quite often. Similarly, the Chinese used a mixture of uncooked tea, sugar, and rice-based on heavy ironworks to the same effect.

Benefits of a Wood Pellet

If you have decided to purchase a wood pellet smoker-grill, you are on the right track in picking the best among the numerous grills available in the market. Cooking with wood pellet smoker-grill offers a ton of advantages; for example, you can cook a range of cuts, meats, and vegetables efficiently and effectively. The wood chips will give your food a wonderful and unique flavor.

1 of the grill's most significant selling points is that it is easy to cook and saves time. These grills are popular because they promise healthy, flavorful, and well-cooked food without

taking a long time. These grills preheat quickly and give you outstanding results without compromising the quality of the food.

Smoking your food is undoubtedly a unique and distinctive way to cook it. The process brightens and enhances the flavor multiple times. The chips added to the grill's hopper lend a rustic and earthy flavor to your meat or vegetables. As the food is being simmered through, it is being flavored effectively, too. Ham, pork, roasts, bacon, beef brisket, whole poultry, and all kinds of fish can quickly be cooked to perfection.

Once you have set the dial temperature or the keypad (depending on the smoker-grill model you have), you are free to check-in (or not at all) as and when required. Some of these models also feature a remote thermometer, which indicates when the optimal temperature has been reached. The smoker's air temperature is increased carefully and slowly to ensure that it is even and perfect.

Temperature regulation is an essential advantage of these kinds of grills. Most people who have manned 1 or another type of traditional grill will swear by the unreliability of heat. It would be fine if you managed the heat depending on the conditions outside. However, with the wood pellet smoker-grill, the temperature can be controlled with the press of a button or a turn of the dial.

Technology and its constant advances allow people to choose from a variety of options. There are small and compact grills that can sit on a small balcony. On the other hand, you can select the largest 1 with the best features to entertain and pamper your family and friends. Similarly, there are technically advanced versions that allow you to cook at the press of a button. So, there's a pattern out there for everyone.

Skills and Techniques to Master

- **Smoking:** it is cooking, seasoning, and flavoring spice by the smoke display from smoldering or burning material, especially wood. Fish, meat, vegetables, and cheese are the most common types of food cooked through smoking methods. Lapsang souchong tea and smoked beer are just some of the examples of smoked beverages.

- **Roasting:** a smoke pit and a masonry oven are similar in that they both allow open flame and use convection in cooking foods. Meat is ideal for roasting and other starchy foods like bread, desserts, and various casseroles. Roasting uses direct and indirect heat to surround the food with hot air in which these foods can be basted, just like the standard grilling method.

- **Braising:** braising can be done using vegetables and meat placed in a pot above the grill. For barbecue braising, an electric or gas charbroil grill is the best choice. Another method is by combining braising and dry heat directly on a ribbed surface for moist heat. The pot needs to be on top of the grill with a cover. Could you leave it to simmer for a few hours? The advantage is that it permits glazing of the meat with sauce and finishing it directly after braising over the fire in which the heart becomes soft-textured and falls quickly off the bone. Before the braising, the meat becomes brown directly on the grill. Braising, in general, is faster than pit-smoking but slower than regular grilling.

- **Searing:** the secret to ensuring great flavor in grilling is the method or the technique used in searing. It caramelizes the meat surface, and unlike what most people believe, it does not lock in moisture. Instead, it makes the meat flavorful and crisp. It works best with any cut of pork, lamb, and beef. To sear, make sure that the grill is scorching before placing the meat on and let it stay there for 1 minute. Then flip the heart and reduce the heat. The high temperature will then caramelize the surface of the meat. Once done, repeat the process until the meat is done.

- **Indirect-grill:** if you want to be a versatile griller, then you have to master the art of indirect grilling. Direct heat is ideal for cooking fast and hot, while indirect grilling is suitable for cooking large roasts and whole chickens and baking bread. To do this, you need to turn off the burners placed directly under the cooking foods. If you are using a multi-burner grill, turn off those in the middle and use those on the sides. Cook the meat first, then move it to indirect heat to roast it slowly. Doing it this way keeps the heart tender and moist without burning the outside.

15

- **Grill-Baking:** it is possible to combine roasting and grilling in cooking meat coated or stuffed with batter or breadcrumbs using a drip pan below the grill surface and a baking sheet pan above the grill surface. Making desserts and casseroles, as well as baking bread, is also possible with grill-baking. When you cook coated and stuffed meat, bake it first on the sheet pan and then place it directly on the grilling surface for char marks. This process cooks the heart twice. The drip pan will then catch any crumbs that fall.

- **Charcoal kettle-grilling:** the method of barbecuing over a charcoal fire in a kettle is called charcoal kettle-grilling. The foods cooked through this method contain charred grill marks, especially on edge. This charcoal-grilled experience is being revived in some restaurants, and they use infrared heat or ceramic lava rocks for cooking the foods in the same manner when charcoal kettle-grilling is used. The foods cooked in this manner are tagged as charcoal-grilled or charcoal cooked on the menu.

Grilling and Barbecue Tips From the Experts

Here is some of the best advice gathered from the experts about the most useful tips in grilling and barbecue for a successful, fun, and delicious BBQ party ever.

Essential Tips in Grilling

1. Rub the grill with non-stick cooking spray or oil to prevent foods from sticking to the grill.

2. To allow smoke penetration and even cooking, leave enough space for foods on the grill.

3. For steaks, when the juice on the uncooked side starts to bubble, turn it. The more well-done the meat, the more precise the liquid that comes out of it. For other meat, turn them on the grill just once.

4. To prevent the sauce from burning, apply the dressing during the last 10 minutes. The sauce should contain brown sugar, honey, and molasses.

5. Flare-ups can blacken your food, so make sure to have a spray bottle handy to quench flare-ups when they occur.

6. Cooked foods should be placed on a clean plate. Avoid using the containers that previously held raw fish, meat, and poultry as these may contain bacteria that will contaminate the cooked food. It may then cause food poisoning.

7. Once done with cooking, brush the grilling surface with a wired brush to remove stuck-on foods.

Tips for Grilling Beef: Perfect Steak

1. Good steaks should be at least 1 inch thick.

2. For boneless steak, allow ½ lb. per person, and for bone-in steaks, allow ¾ lbs. per person.

3. Keep the steak from curling on the grill, trim off fat to at least 1/8 inch and make sure the edges are scored.

4. Turn the steaks only when the juices start to bubble on the uncooked side of the grill.

5. Less time is required to grill the second side of the steak than the first.

6. After turning, add or season with salt and pepper each browned side of the steak.

7. In grilling, the grill surface must be at 350° C, and the steak should be cooked for 20 minutes if it needs to be rare, 25 minutes for medium-rare, and more than 25 minutes if it should be well done.

Tips for Grilling Chicken

1. Before grilling, it is best if the chicken is marinated or basted with oil.

2. To keep quarters and halves flat on the grill while grilling, break the joints and grill similar sized pieces.

3. Lay the chicken skin-side up on the grill.

4. When juices that flow are already evident, and when the joints can be moved easily, the chicken is done already.

5. Breasts should be grilled at approximately 375° C, and quarters or halves should be examined at 350°.

6. Even cooking is quite tricky when grilling split halves of chicken. The secret is to place the darker meat towards or on the hottest part of your 2-zone

grill. The chicken will then cook consistently, while the white meat will not dry out quickly.

7. To keep the chicken's original golden color, paint the chicken with yellow mustard before applying the rub as the rub is challenging to affix and can remove the stain. By painting yellow mustard on the chicken, the rub will not only stick to the chicken, but the color will be very appealing when the chicken is cooked.

8. You can also add rosemary, parsley, or basil to the chicken before grilling to add some extra zip.

Tips for Grilling Seafood

1. For grilling, choose the fish with thick meat such as shark, salmon, tuna, or swordfish.

2. Fillets should be cut at least 1 inch because if it is thinner, it will quickly dry out when grilled.

3. Fish won't stick if the grill is clean so make sure to clean it first before grilling.

4. Oil the grill surface with olive oil for better results.

5. To prevent the fish from breaking apart, use a spatula when turning the fish.

6. Vegetables and fish don't need to be tenderized so when marinating, make sure to not leave them for too long and not more than a few hours. On the other hand, chicken, pork, lamb, and beef are best

marinated for a few hours to overnight for maximum flavors.

Tips for Grilling Pork

1. Pork cuts need to be at least 1–1 ½ inch thick.

2. When the meat is no longer pink along the bone, and the juice that flows is clear, that means the pork is done.

3. Fresh veggies add variety to meals, so add some and then brush with some marinade, and you can now skewer and grill.

Tips for Grilling Vegetables

1. Parboil starchy or substantial vegetables before threading them onto the skewers for grilling so they can be evenly cooked.

Wrap some vegetables in foil and cook them on the grill and apply them every once in a while, to deter them from even cooking.

MEAT IDEAS

Rib Tips & Techniques

1. Remove the membrane. That weird membrane on the back of ribs (sometimes called silver skin) can make them harder to pull off the bone and less tender. To get pit master-level results each time, remove it.

2. Use mustard as a binder. Mustard works excellent as a binder for your rub on fatty meats such as ribs. Rub plain yellow mustard or another smooth mustard over your ribs before or after your rub. It will keep your rub on your heart and not all over your drip pan.

3. Use whatever liquid you like best (including beer or wine, but not liquor) for your spritz or your wrap. When watching a competition cook prep ribs with Mountain Dew, I asked why. "It's what my brother and I like and what we had, so we just started using it," he told me. I use Pepsi; my dad and brother use apple juice. Use what you like, see what other pitmasters are using and try that for a change. It's a great place to experiment.

21

4. Sauce it—just don't overdo it. Again, saucing is a real preference. At parties, I always have a plate of ribs with just a dry rub. Over the years, my ribs have gone from dry to heavily sauced, and now I only use a light sweet coating. As you will see in the recipes, we also have other ways to achieve sweetness.

5. Country-style ribs are ribs. Cook boneless country-style ribs the same way you would other ribs. The smoked flavor is excellent, and they are incredibly tender when done.

Pork Shoulder Tips & Techniques

1. Inject your pork shoulder for extra moisture and flavor. Using a tea, as we will learn to make in the recipe section, inject your shoulder. A right shoulder will have a nice flavorful bark (see the next tip), but injecting will give it flavor everywhere.

2. Smoke your pork longer for a good "bark." The bark isn't just on trees or what your dog does. The bark is that delicious crust on the outside of well-smoked meat. The bark develops when the heart and rub combined with uninterrupted smoke for an extended period. A right pork shoulder will have a good, dark bark. To increase the amount of bark, smoke the pork longer, unwrapped.

3. Use your hands when pulling the meat—it's easier. There are some new cool claws available that can be used for pulling pork. They keep your hands

from getting hot and greasy. Fact is, though, with those, the pull never really feels right. I have a pair of cheap cotton gloves I wear under food service gloves. The gloves keep my hands from burning but let me pull the meat precisely as I like it.

Whole Chicken Tips & Techniques

1. Rub your chicken with oil as well as seasoning. It helps work in the rub but also produces a more golden skin.

2. Injecting a whole chicken with liquid can change it from pedestrian to something that can only be described as excellent. Use a tea made from your favorite seasoning or even butter to inject your chicken with before cooking. Injecting ads flavor and keeps your chicken moist.

3. When you rub your chicken, get the rub between the skin and the breast meat. Just be mindful not to rip the skin much when doing this. As someone who loves white meat but won't eat the skin, I can tell you this is a great way to add flavor.

Turkey Tips & Techniques

1. Baste your turkey with butter. It is certainly not the healthiest way of cooking it, but it is the tastiest, in my opinion. Just leave the stick on your side table and rub the turkey with it as it cooks and becomes more golden.

2. Use your thermometer. Those built-in ones, the little red buttons, just don't work in a grill or smoker.

3. Don't put a stuffed turkey on the grill. Unfortunately, it's hard to make sure your turkey and stuffing are done at the same time — and I'm sorry, but moist turkey is too good to waste on even the best filling.

Lambchop Tips & Techniques

1. Lamb chops are perfect with a reverse sear. Again, I like this best on a grill with some kind of open flame option, but if yours doesn't, grab your cast-iron skillet instead and sear the chops at 400° F for about 2 minutes per side.

2. Mince your herbs for lamb chops and rub them into your meat. I like to use olive oil to help me rub the seasonings all over the chops, not just in 1 area.

3. Go slightly overboard on the black pepper. The pepper gives your lamb a little kick.

Salmon Tips & Techniques

1. Use a cedar plank for smoking and barbecuing salmon. Cooking with a cedar plank allows the wood's flavor and moisture to be passed directly to the salmon. Cedar planks are so standard today you can find them at many local grocery stores or Walmart.

2. Suppose you do grill salmon directly on the grate, oil the grates beforehand. Even on porcelain grates, fish skin likes to stick, and it stinks the second time you cook it.

3. Hit the meat of the fish with an open flame after smoking. Only do this if you can and for a concise amount of time. Also, be careful that your salmon doesn't flake apart while doing this. Your big spatula is critical here.

4. Use mayonnaise or Dijon mustard to keep salmon moist. Applying a thin coat of mayonnaise or mustard to your salmon before cooking it will keep the fish from drying out, and I swear it won't taste weird at all.

Tuna Tips & Techniques

1. Try a reverse sear on tuna for a slight smoke flavor. I don't smoke tuna steaks as long as other fish—less than 30 minutes.

2. Dill is excellent on tuna like it is on most seafood. I use dill weed a lot on seafood, but it is best on tuna steaks. Sprinkle on a generous amount for great flavor.

3. Be careful not to overcook the fish. Tuna can go from unusual to cat food fast if you're not careful. It is steaks; treat them as such. Err on the side of rare, especially if using sushi-grade tuna. You can always put it back on the grill if it's not done enough for whoever is eating it.

Shrimp Tips & Techniques

1. My favorite shrimp is Cajun or Creole Louisiana-style shrimp, but there are all kinds of ways to prepare shrimp on your pellet grill. Just like any other meat we cook; we never feel bound to any 1 style of cooking. Experimenting makes us all better pitmasters.

2. Lemon is an excellent complement to shrimp. Use it in the cooking or after for squeezing.

Grill baskets are worth their price and great for cooking shrimp. Pick 1 up and cook your shrimp over a direct flame or straight on the grill

MARINATE

1. Prepare meat according to the recipe. Sometimes meat is cured, marinated, or simply seasoned with the rub. These preparation methods ensure smoked meat turns out flavorful, tender, and incredibly juicy.

2. Brine is a solution to treating poultry, pork, or ham. It involves dissolving brine ingredients in water poured into an enormous container and then adding meat. Then let soak for at minimum 8 hours and after that, rinse it well and pat dry before you begin smoking.

3. Marinate treat beef or briskets and add flavors to it. It's better to make deep cuts in meat to let marinate ingredients deep into it. Drain meat or smoke it straightaway.

4. Rubs are commonly used to treat beef, poultry, or ribs. They are a combination of salt and many spices, rubbed generously all over the meat. Then the meat is left to rest for at least 2 hours or more before smoking it.

5. Before smoking meat, make sure it is at room temperature. It ensures the meat is cooked evenly and reaches its internal temperature at the end of smoking time.

SAUCES

1. BBQ Sauce

Preparation time: 5 minutes.

Cooking time: 10 minutes.

Servings: 1 batch.

Ingredients:

- ✓ 1 cup applesauce.

- ✓ 1/2 cup ketchup.

- ✓ 2 cups unpacked brown sugar.

- ✓ ¼ cup lemon juice.

- ✓ 2 tbsp. hot chili powder.

- ✓ 1 tbsp. jalapeno powder.

- ✓ 1 tbsp. celery seed (ground).

- ✓ 1 tbsp. oregano.

- ✓ 1 tbsp. ginger (ground).

- ✓ 2 tbsp. dill seeds (ground).

- ✓ 2 tbsp. black pepper.

- ✓ 1 tbsp. salt.

Preparation:

1. In a large saucepan, mix your ingredients.

2. Bring mixture to a boil, then reduce heat to low and simmer for 10 minutes. Cool before serving.

Nutrition:

- Calories: 45.
- Fat: 0 g.
- Sodium: 200 mg.
- Carbohydrates: 14 g.
- Fiber: 0 g.
- Sugars: 8 g.

2. Goblin Barter Sauce

Preparation time: 3 minutes.

Cooking time: 10 minutes.

Servings: 2 cups.

Ingredients:

- ✓ 2 cups ketchup.
- ✓ ¼ cup molasses.
- ✓ 1 cup maple syrup.
- ✓ ¼ cup Worcestershire sauce.
- ✓ 2 tsp. white pepper.
- ✓ 2 tbsp. garlic salt.
- ✓ 2 tbsp. pumpkin pie spice.
- ✓ 1 tbsp. cilantro.
- ✓ 2 tbsp. nacho chili powder.
- ✓ 2 tbsp. black pepper.
- ✓ 1 tbsp. sea salt/kosher salt.

Preparation:

1. In a large saucepan, mix your ingredients.
2. Bring mixture to a boil, then reduce heat to low and simmer for 10 minutes. Cool before serving.

Nutrition:

- Calories: 43.
- Fat: 0 g.
- Sodium: 196 mg.
- Carbohydrates: 16 g.
- Fiber: 0 g.
- Sugars: 10 g.

3. Kung-Fu BBQ Sauce

Preparation time: 5 minutes.

Cooking time: 10 minutes.

Servings: 1 cup.

Ingredients:

- ✓ 2 tbsp. butter.
- ✓ 1 medium onion, finely chopped.
- ✓ 2 cloves garlic, minced.
- ✓ ½ cup orange juice.
- ✓ 1 cup ketchup.
- ✓ 1 cup cider vinegar.
- ✓ 3 tbsp. all-purpose seafood seasoning.
- ✓ 4 tbsp. hot chili powder.
- ✓ 3 tbsp. granulated chicken bouillon.
- ✓ 1 tbsp. mustard seed (ground).
- ✓ 1 tbsp. oregano.
- ✓ 2 tbsp. dry nacho seasoning.
- ✓ 1 tbsp. all-purpose chicken seasoning.
- ✓ 2 tbsp. black pepper.
- ✓ 2 tbsp. sea salt/kosher salt.

Preparation:

1. In a large saucepan, mix your ingredients.

2. Bring mixture to a boil, then reduce heat to low and simmer for 10 minutes. Cool before serving.

Nutrition:

- Calories: 35.

- Fat: 0 g.

- Sodium: 150 mg.

- Carbohydrates: 18 g.

- Fiber: 0 g.

- Sugars: 10 g

4. Windy City Street Fighter Sauce

Preparation time: 3 minutes.

Cooking time: 10 minutes.

Servings: 2

Ingredients:

- ✓ 1 (18 oz.) bottle barbeque sauce.
- ✓ 2 tbsp. whiskey.
- ✓ 1 tbsp. Worcestershire sauce.
- ✓ 2 tbsp. allspice powder.
- ✓ 4 tbsp. hot curry powder.
- ✓ 1 tbsp. all-purpose seafood seasoning.
- ✓ 3 tbsp. Hungarian sweet paprika.
- ✓ 1 tbsp. lemon pepper.
- ✓ 2 tbsp. mustard seed (ground).

Preparation:

3. In a large saucepan, mix your ingredients.

4. Bring mixture to a boil, then reduce heat to low and simmer for 10 minutes. Cool before serving.

Nutrition:

- Calories: 38.
- Fat: 0 g.
- Sodium: 196 mg.
- Carbohydrates: 14 g.
- Fiber: 0 g.
- Sugars: 8 g.

5. Mordor BBQ Sauce

Preparation time: 3 minutes.

Cooking time: 10 minutes.

Servings: 1

Ingredients:

- ✓ 1 cup Coca Cola.
- ✓ 1 cup canned tomato sauce.
- ✓ 1 (6 oz.) can tomato paste.
- ✓ ½ cup Worcestershire sauce.
- ✓ ½ cup packed brown sugar.
- ✓ ½ cup molasses.
- ✓ ½ cup cider vinegar.
- ✓ 2 tbsp. nacho chili powder.
- ✓ 2 tbsp. garlic powder.
- ✓ 2 tbsp. onion powder.
- ✓ 2 tbsp. celery seed (ground).
- ✓ 2 tbsp. ground cumin.
- ✓ 2 tbsp. sea salt/kosher salt.

Preparation:

1. In a large saucepan, mix your ingredients.

2. Bring mixture to a boil, then reduce heat to low and simmer for 10 minutes. Cool before serving.

Nutrition:

- Calories: 27.
- Fat: 0 g.
- Sodium: 157 mg.
- Carbohydrates: 14 g.
- Fiber: 0 g.
- Sugars: 8 g.

6. Guardhouse Sauce

Preparation time: 3 minutes.

Cooking time: 10 minutes.

Servings: 1

Ingredients:

- ✓ ½ cup orange juice.
- ✓ ½ cup cider vinegar.
- ✓ ¼ cup red wine.
- ✓ ¼ cup soy sauce.
- ✓ 2 tbsp. red pepper flakes.
- ✓ 2 tbsp. all-purpose beef seasoning.
- ✓ 2 tbsp. bacon bits.
- ✓ 1 tbsp. Cajun seasoning.
- ✓ 1 tbsp. ginger (ground).
- ✓ 1 tbsp. coriander seed (ground).
- ✓ 1 tbsp. sea salt/kosher salt.

Preparation:

1. In a large saucepan, mix your ingredients.
2. Bring mixture to a boil, then reduce heat to low and simmer for 10 minutes. Cool before serving.

Nutrition:

- Calories: 37.

- Fat: 0 g.

- Sodium: 168 mg.

- Carbohydrates: 20 g.

- Fiber: 0 g.

- Sugars: 9 g.

7. Steindorff Sweet Sauce

Preparation time: 3 minutes.

Cooking time: 10 minutes.

Servings: 2

Ingredients:

- ✓ 1 (28 oz.) bottle ketchup.
- ✓ 2 cups honey.
- ✓ 2 cups molasses.
- ✓ 1 cup white sugar.
- ✓ 1 (12 oz.) jar hoisin sauce.
- ✓ 1 (10 oz.) bottle oyster sauce.
- ✓ 3 tbsp. oregano.
- ✓ 4 tbsp. pumpkin pie spice.
- ✓ 2 tbsp. red pepper flakes.
- ✓ 4 tbsp. gram masala.
- ✓ 2 tbsp. Mexican oregano.
- ✓ 1 tbsp. garlic powder.
- ✓ 1 tbsp. black pepper.
- ✓ 1 tbsp. sea salt/kosher salt.

Preparation:

1. In a large saucepan, mix your ingredients.

2. Bring mixture to a boil, then reduce heat to low and simmer for 10 minutes. Cool before serving.

Nutrition:

- Calories: 67.

- Fat: 0 g.

- Sodium: 135 mg.

- Carbohydrates: 14 g.

- Fiber: 0 g.

- Sugars: 10 g.

8. Keera-Keera

Preparation time: 3 minutes.

Cooking time: 10 minutes.

Servings: 2

Ingredients:

- ✓ 2 cups ketchup.
- ✓ 2 cups tomato sauce.
- ✓ 1¼ cups brown sugar.
- ✓ 1¼ cups red wine vinegar.
- ✓ ½ cup molasses.
- ✓ 2 tbsp. hickory-flavored liquid smoke.
- ✓ 2 tbsp. all-purpose Greek seasoning.
- ✓ 1 tbsp. cloves (ground).
- ✓ 3 tbsp. paprika.
- ✓ 3 tbsp. taco seasoning.
- ✓ 1 tbsp. onion powder.
- ✓ 1 tbsp. black pepper.
- ✓ 2 tbsp. sea salt/kosher salt.

Preparation:

1. In a large saucepan, mix your ingredients.

2. Bring mixture to a boil, then reduce heat to low and simmer for 10 minutes. Cool before serving.

Nutrition:

- Calories: 45.

- Fat: 0 g.

- Sodium: 200 mg.

- Carbohydrates: 14 g.

- Fiber: 0 g.

- Sugars: 8 g.

9. Joker Sauce

Preparation time: 3 minutes.

Cooking time: 10 minutes.

Servings: 1

Ingredients:

- ¾ cup bourbon whiskey.
- 2 cups ketchup.
- ¼ cup tomato paste.
- ½ cup cider vinegar.
- 2 tbsp. liquid smoke.
- ¼ cup Worcestershire sauce.
- ¼ cup brown sugar.
- 2 tbsp. dill seeds (ground).
- 2 tbsp. unsweetened cocoa powder.
- 1 tbsp. oregano.
- 3 tbsp. granulated beef bouillon.
- 1 tbsp. mace (ground).
- 2 tbsp. black pepper.

Preparation:

1. In a large saucepan, mix your ingredients.
2. Bring mixture to a boil, then reduce heat to low and simmer for 10 minutes. Cool before serving.

Nutrition:

- Calories: 67.

- Fat: 0 g.

- Sodium: 198 mg.

- Carbohydrates: 10 g.

- Fiber: 0 g.

- Sugars: 9 g.

10. Korean Cyclops Sauce

Preparation time: 3 minutes.

Cooking time: 10 minutes.

Servings: 2

Ingredients:

- ✓ 1 cup soy sauce.
- ✓ ¾ cup dark brown sugar.
- ✓ 2 tbsp. minced garlic.
- ✓ 1 tbsp. rice wine vinegar.
- ✓ 1 tbsp. chili-garlic sauce.
- ✓ 2 tbsp. coffee beans (ground).
- ✓ 2 tbsp. all-purpose seafood seasoning.
- ✓ 2 tbsp. Chinese 5-spice powder.
- ✓ 1 tbsp. ginger.
- ✓ 1 tbsp. black pepper.

Preparation:

1. In a large saucepan, mix your ingredients.

2. Bring mixture to a boil, then reduce heat to low and simmer for 10 minutes. Cool before serving.

Nutrition:

- Calories: 38.
- Fat: 0 g.
- Sodium: 150 mg.
- Carbohydrates: 20 g.
- Fiber: 0 g.
- Sugars: 10 g.

11. Operation Overlord

Preparation time: 3 minutes.

Cooking time: 10 minutes.

Servings: 2

Ingredients:

- ✓ 2 cups apple cider vinegar.
- ✓ ½ cup ketchup.
- ✓ 1 cup brown sugar.
- ✓ 3 tbsp. hot chili powder.
- ✓ 1 tbsp. granulated beef bouillon.
- ✓ 2 tbsp. gram masala.
- ✓ 3 tbsp. burrito seasoning mix.
- ✓ 2 tbsp. habanero powder.
- ✓ 2 tbsp. parsley.
- ✓ 2 tbsp. sea salt/kosher salt.

Preparation:

1. In a large saucepan, mix your ingredients.

2. Bring mixture to a boil, then reduce heat to low and simmer for 10 minutes. Cool before serving.

Nutrition:

- Calories: 28.

- Fat: 0 g.

- Sodium: 167 mg.

- Carbohydrates: 12 g.

- Fiber: 0 g.

- Sugars: 10 g.

BEEF RECIPES

12. Pellet Grill Meatloaf

Preparation time: 30 minutes.

Cooking time: 6 hours.

Servings: 8

Ingredients:

- ✓ 1 cup breadcrumbs.
- ✓ 2 lbs. ground beef.
- ✓ ¼ lb. ground sausage.
- ✓ 2 large eggs (beaten).
- ✓ 2 garlic cloves (grated).
- ✓ ½ tsp. ground black pepper.
- ✓ ¼ tsp. red pepper flakes.
- ✓ ½ tsp. salt or to taste.
- ✓ 1 tsp. dried parsley.
- ✓ 1 green onion (chopped).
- ✓ 1 tsp. paprika.
- ✓ ½ tsp. Italian seasoning.
- ✓ 1 small onion (chopped).
- ✓ 1 cup milk.
- ✓ 1 cup BBQ sauce.
- ✓ ½ cup apple juice.

Preparation:

1. Preheat the grill to 225° F with the lid closed for 15 minutes, using apple pellet.

2. In a large mixing bowl, combine the egg, milk, parsley, onion, green onion, paprika, Italian seasoning, breadcrumbs, ground beef, ground sausage, salt, pepper flakes, black pepper, and garlic. Mix thoroughly until the ingredients are well combined.

3. Form the mixture into a loaf and wrap the loaf loosely in tin foil and use a knife to poke some holes in the foil. The holes will allow the smoke flavor to enter the loaf.

4. Place the wrapped loaf on the grill grate and grill for 1 hour 30 minutes.

5. Meanwhile, combine the BBQ sauce and apple juice in a mixing bowl.

6. Tear off the top half of the tin foil to apply the glaze. Apply the glaze over the meatloaf. Continue grilling until the internal temperature of the meatloaf is 160° F.

7. Remove the meatloaf from the grill and let it sit for a few minutes to cool.

8. Cut and serve.

Nutrition:

- Carbohydrates: 22 g.

- Protein: 28 g.

- Fat: 6 g.

- Sodium: 1213 mg.

- Cholesterol: 81 mg.

13. BBQ Brisket

Preparation time: 30 minutes.

Cooking time: 6 hours.

Servings: 8

Ingredients:

- ✓ 1 (12–14) packer beef brisket.
- ✓ 1 tsp. cayenne pepper.
- ✓ 1 tsp. cumin.
- ✓ 2 tbsp. paprika.
- ✓ 1 tbsp. smoked paprika.
- ✓ 1 tbsp. onion powder.
- ✓ 1/2 tbsp. maple sugar.
- ✓ 2 tsp. ground black pepper.
- ✓ 2 tsp. kosher salt.

Preparation:

1. Combine all the ingredients except the brisket in a mixing bowl.

2. Season all sides of the brisket with the seasoning mixture as needed and wrap the brisket in a plastic wrap. Refrigerate for 12 hours or more.

3. Unwrap the brisket and let it sit for about 2 hours or until the brisket is at room temperature.

4. Preheat the pellet grill to 225° F with lid close, using mesquite or oak wood pellet.

5. Place the brisket on the grill grate and grill for about 6 hours. Remove the brisket from the grill and wrap with foil.

6. Return brisket to the grill and cook for about 4 hours or until the brisket's temperature reaches 204° F.

7. Remove the brisket from the grill and let it sit for about 40 minutes to cool.

8. Unwrap the brisket and cut it into slices.

Nutrition:

- Carbohydrates: 22 g.

- Protein: 28 g.

- Fat: 6 g.

- Sodium: 1213 mg.

- Cholesterol: 81 mg.

14. Tri-Tip Roast

Preparation time: 30 minutes.

Cooking time: 50 minutes.

Servings: 8

Ingredients:

- ✓ 2 lbs. tri-tip roast (silver skin and the fat cap removed).
- ✓ 1 tsp. salt.
- ✓ 1 tsp. ground black pepper.
- ✓ ½ tsp. paprika.
- ✓ 1 tsp. fresh rosemary.
- ✓ 1 tsp. garlic powder.
- ✓ 1 tbsp. olive oil.

Preparation:

1. Combine salt, pepper, garlic, paprika, and rosemary.

2. Brush the tri-tip generously with olive oil. Season the roast with seasoning mixture generously.

3. Preheat the grill smoker 225° F with the lid closed for 15 minutes, using hickory, mesquite, or oak wood pellet.

4. Place the tri-tip roast on the grill grate directly and cook for about 1 hour or until the tri tip's temperature reaches 135° F.

5. Remove the tri-tip from the grill and wrap it with heavy-duty foil. Set aside in a cooler.

6. Adjust the grill temperature to high and preheat with lid closed for 15 minutes.

7. Remove the tri-tip from the foil and place it on the grill cook for 8 minutes, turning the tri-tip after the first 4 minutes.

8. Remove the tri-tip from the grill and let it rest for a few minutes to cool.

9. Cut them into slices against the grain and serve.

Nutrition:

- Carbohydrates: 22 g.
- Protein: 28 g.
- Fat: 6 g.
- Sodium: 13 mg.
- Cholesterol: 81 mg.

15. Baby Back Rib

Preparation time: 30 minutes.

Cooking time: 5 hours.

Servings: 8

Ingredients:

- ✓ ½ cup BBQ sauce.
- ✓ 1 rack baby back ribs.
- ✓ 1 cup apple cider.
- ✓ 1 tbsp. Worcestershire sauce.
- ✓ 1 tsp. paprika.
- ✓ ½ cup packed dark brown sugar.
- ✓ 2 tbsp. yellow mustard.
- ✓ 2 tbsp. honey.
- ✓ 2 tbsp. BBQ rub.

Preparation:

1. Remove the membrane on the back of the rib with a butter knife.

2. Combine the mustard, paprika, ½ cup apple cider, and Worcestershire sauce.

3. Rub the mixture over the rib and season the rib with BBQ rub.

4. Start your grill on the smoke setting and leave the lid opened until the fire starts.

5. Close the lid and preheat the grill to 180° F using a hickory wood pellet.

6. Place the rib on the grill, smoke side up. Smoke for 3 hours.

7. Remove the ribs from the grill.

8. Tear off 2 large pieces of heavy-duty aluminum foil and place 1 on a large working surface. Place the rib on the foil, rib side up.

9. Sprinkle the sugar over the rib. Top it with honey and the remaining apple cider.

10. Place the other piece of foil over the rib and crimp the edges of the aluminum foil pieces together to form an airtight seal.

11. Place the sealed rib on the grill and cook for 2 hours.

12. After the cooking cycle, gently remove the foil from the rib and discard it.

13. Brush all sides of the baby back rib with the BBQ sauce.

14. Return the rib to the grill grate directly and cook for an additional 30 minutes or until the sauce coating is firm and thick.

15. Remove the rib from the grill and let it cool for a few minutes.

16. Cut into sizes and serve.

Nutrition:

- Carbohydrates: 22 g.
- Protein: 28 g.
- Fat: 6 g.
- Sodium: 13 mg.
- Cholesterol: 81 mg.

16. Beef Jerky

Preparation time: 30 minutes.

Cooking time: 6 hours.

Servings: 8

Ingredients:

- ✓ 1 cup pineapple juice.
- ✓ ½ cup brown sugar.
- ✓ 2 tbsp. sriracha.
- ✓ 2 tbsp. onion powder.
- ✓ 2 tbsp. minced garlic.
- ✓ 2 tbsp. rice wine vinegar.
- ✓ 2 tbsp. hoisin.
- ✓ 1 tbsp. salt.
- ✓ 1 tbsp. red pepper flakes.
- ✓ 1 tbsp. coarsely ground black pepper.
- ✓ 2 cups coconut amino.
- ✓ 2 jalapeños (thinly sliced).

Meat:

- ✓ 3 lbs. trimmed sirloin steak (sliced to ¼ inch thick).

Preparation:

1. Combine all the marinade ingredients in a mixing bowl and mix until the ingredients are well combined.

2. Put the sliced sirloin in a gallon-sized zip-lock bag and pour the marinade into the bag. Massage the marinade into the beef. Seal the bag and refrigerate for 8 hours.

3. Remove the zip-lock bag from the refrigerator.

4. Activate the pellet grill smoker setting and leave lip opened for 5 minutes until the fire starts.

5. Close the lid and preheat your pellet grill to 180° F, using a hickory pellet.

6. Remove the beef slices from the marinade and pat them dry with a paper towel.

7. Arrange the beef slice on the grill in a single layer. Smoke the beef for about 4–5 hours, turning often after the first 2 hours of smoking. The jerky should be dark and dry when it is done.

8. Remove the jerky from the grill and let it sit for about 1 hour to cool.

9. Serve immediately or store in an airtight container and refrigerate for future use.

Nutrition:

- Carbohydrates: 12 g.

- Protein: 28 g.

- Fat: 16 g.

- Sodium: 23 mg.

- Cholesterol: 21 mg.

17. Beef Skewers

Preparation time: 30 minutes.

Cooking time: 5 hours.

Servings: 8

Ingredients:

- ✓ 2 tbsp. olive oil.

- ✓ 2 lbs. top round steak (cut to ¼-inch-thick and 2-inch-wide slices).

- ✓ 2 garlic cloves (finely chopped).

- ✓ ¼ cup water.

- ✓ ½ cup soy sauce.

- ✓ ¾ cup brown sugar.

- ✓ 1 tbsp. minced fresh ginger.

- ✓ 1 tsp. freshly ground black pepper or more to taste.

- ✓ 3 tbsp. red wine vinegar.

- ✓ 3 tbsp. dried basil.

- ✓ Wooden or bamboo skewers (soaked in water for 30 minutes, at least).

Preparation:

1. In a mixing bowl, combine the olive oil, sugar, ginger, garlic, soy sauce, water, vinegar, pepper, and basil. Mix until the ingredients are well combined.

2. Pour the marinade into a zip-lock bag and add the steak slices. Massage the marinade into the steak slices. Refrigerate for 12 hours or more.

3. Remove the steak slices from the marinade and pat them dry with a paper towel.

4. Thread the steak slices onto the soaked skewers.

5. Activate the smoke setting on your wood smoker grill, using a hickory wood pellet. Leave the lid open until the fire is established.

6. Close the lid and preheat the grill to 325° F for direct-heat cooking.

7. Arrange the skewered steak onto the grill and grill for 8 minutes or until the meat is done, turning occasionally.

8. Remove the skewered meat from the grill and let them sit for a few minutes to cool.

9. Serve warm and enjoy.

Nutrition:

- Carbohydrates: 12 g.

- Protein: 28 g.

- Fat: 16 g.

- Sodium: 23 mg.

- Cholesterol: 21 mg.

18. Smoked Italian Meatballs

Preparation time: 10 minutes.

Cooking time: 30 minutes.

Servings: 8

Ingredients:

- ✓ 1-lb. ground beef.
- ✓ 1-lb. Italian Sausage.
- ✓ ½ cup Italian breadcrumbs.
- ✓ 1 tsp. dry mustard.
- ✓ ½ cup parmesan cheese (grated).
- ✓ 1 tsp. Italian seasoning.
- ✓ 1 jalapeño (finely chopped).
- ✓ 2 eggs.
- ✓ 1 tsp. salt.
- ✓ 1 onion (finely chopped).
- ✓ 2 tsp. garlic powder.
- ✓ ½ tsp. smoked paprika.
- ✓ 1 tsp. oregano.
- ✓ 1 tsp. crushed red pepper.
- ✓ 1 tbsp. Worcestershire sauce.

Preparation:

1. Combine all the ingredients in a large mixing bowl. Mix until the ingredients are well combined.

2. Mold the mixture into 1 ½ inch balls and arrange the balls into a greased baking sheet.

3. Preheat the wood pellet smoker to 180° F, using hickory pellet.

4. Arrange the meatballs on the grill and smoke for 20 minutes.

5. Increase the griller's temperature to 350° F and smoke until the internal temperature of the meatballs reaches 165° F.

6. Remove the meatballs from the grill and let them cool for a few minutes.

7. Serve warm and enjoy.

Nutrition:

- Carbohydrates: 12 g.

- Protein: 28 g.

- Fat: 16 g.

- Sodium: 23 mg.

- Cholesterol: 21 mg.

19. Prime Rib Roast

Preparation time: 30 minutes.

Cooking time: 5 hours.

Servings: 8

Ingredients:

- ✓ 6 lbs. boneless prime rib roast.
- ✓ 2 tsp. salt or more to taste.
- ✓ 2 tsp. ground black pepper or more to taste.
- ✓ ½ cup olive oil.
- ✓ 1/8 cup red wine vinegar.
- ✓ 2 cups low sodium beef broth.
- ✓ 1 tsp. thyme.
- ✓ 6 garlic cloves (minced).
- ✓ 2 tsp. fresh rosemary.

BBQ rub:

- ✓ ½ cup brown sugar.
- ✓ ½ tsp. cayenne pepper.
- ✓ 1 tbsp. garlic powder.
- ✓ 1 tbsp. smoked paprika.
- ✓ 2 tsp. paprika.
- ✓ 1 tsp. mustard powder.

✓ 1 tsp. onion powder.　　　✓ 1 tbsp. kosher salt.

✓ 1 tbsp. black pepper.

Preparation:

1. Combine the garlic, thyme, rosemary, vinegar, oil, pepper, and salt.

2. Pour the mixture into a zip-lock bag and add the prime roast. Refrigerate for about 6 hours or overnight.

3. Before roasting, remove the rib roast from the marinade and let it sit for about 2 hours or until it is at room temperature.

4. Meanwhile, combine all the ingredients for the rub in a mixing bowl.

5. Season all sides of the rib with enough rub. Store the remaining rub in an airtight container for future use.

6. Place a v-shaped rack in a roasting pan and pour the beef broth into the bottom of the pan. Place the rib roast on the rack, fat side up.

7. Preheat your pellet grill on high heat with lid closed for 15 minutes. Use mesquite wood pellets.

8. Place the roasting pan on the grill. Roast for 30 minutes.

9. Reduce the heat to 250° F and roast for an additional 3 hours or until the rib roast's temperature reaches 130° F.

10. Remove the pan from the grill and let the roast sit for a few minutes to cool.

11. Transfer the roast to a cutting board and cut into sizes.

Nutrition:

- Carbohydrates: 12 g.
- Protein: 28 g.
- Fat: 16 g.
- Sodium: 23 mg.
- Cholesterol: 21 mg.

20. Beef Tenderloin

Preparation time: 10 minutes.

Cooking time: 30 minutes.

Servings: 8

Ingredients:

- ✓ 4 lbs. beef tenderloin.
- ✓ 1 tbsp. olive oil.
- ✓ ½ tsp. paprika.
- ✓ 2 tsp. Jacobsen salt.
- ✓ ½ tsp. ground cumin.
- ✓ 1 tsp. red pepper flakes.
- ✓ 1 tsp. ground black pepper.
- ✓ 1 tsp. fresh thyme.
- ✓ ½ tsp. oregano.

Mustard cream sauce:

- ✓ 1 tsp. freshly ground black pepper.
- ✓ 1 tsp. oil.
- ✓ 1 cup heavy cream.
- ✓ ¼ cup shallot (chopped).
- ✓ 2 tsp. chopped fresh basil.
- ✓ 2 tsp. chopped fresh dill.
- ✓ 1 garlic clove (minced).

- ✓ 1 cup dry white wine.
- ✓ 4 tbsp. mustard.
- ✓ 1 tsp. Jacobsen salt.

Preparation:

1. In a small mixing bowl, combine the thyme, oregano, pepper flakes, black pepper, cumin, salt, paprika, and oregano.

2. Rub all sides of the tenderloin with olive oil.

3. Sprinkle rub mixture over the tenderloin as needed. Make sure the tenderloin is coated in seasonings.

4. Preheat your pellet smoker grill on high with lid closed. Use apple or maple wood pellet.

5. Place tenderloin on the grill grate and cook for about 15 minutes.

6. Reduce the grill temperature to 375° F and cook for an additional 30 minutes or until the tenderloin's temperature reaches 130° F.

7. Remove the tenderloin from heat and let it rest for a few minutes to cool.

8. For the mustard sauce, heat the olive oil in a saucepan over medium to high heat.

9. Add the shallot and garlic. Sauté until the veggies are tender.

10. Stir in the mustard, black pepper, and wine.

11. Bring to a boil, reduce the heat and simmer until the sauce thickens, stirring often.

12. Remove the saucepan from heat and stir in the heavy cream, basil, dill, salt, and pepper.

13. Cut the tenderloin into sizes and serve with mustard sauce.

Nutrition:

- Carbohydrates: 12 g.

- Protein: 28 g.

- Fat: 16 g.

- Sodium: 23 mg.

- Cholesterol: 21 mg.

21. Beef Stuffed Bell Pepper

Preparation time: 10 minutes.

Cooking time: 30 minutes.

Servings: 8

Ingredients:

- ✓ 4 large red bell pepper.
- ✓ ½ cups cooked rice.
- ✓ 1 small onion (diced).
- ✓ 1 tsp. chili powder.
- ✓ 1 tomato (finely chopped).
- ✓ 1 tsp. olive oil.
- ✓ ¼ tsp. ground black pepper or to taste.
- ✓ ¼ tsp. red pepper flakes.
- ✓ ½ tsp. salt.
- ✓ ¼ tsp. garlic.
- ✓ 1-lb. ground beef.
- ✓ 1 cup shredded parmesan cheese.
- ✓ 4 tbsp. ketchup.
- ✓ ½ cup dry quick oats.

Preparation:

1. Cut off the top of the pepper and scoop out the pepper membrane and seeds.

2. Heat up the olive oil in a large skillet over medium to high heat. Add the onion and sliced tomatoes. Sauté until the onion is tender.

3. Add the ground beef and cook until the ground beef is pink, breaking the beef apart while cooking.

4. Remove the skillet from heat and stir in the salt, garlic, ketchup, pepper, rice, oat, pepper flakes, and chili powder.

5. Start the grill on a smoker mode and leave it open for 5 minutes or until the fire has started.

6. Close the lid and preheat it to 350° F, using mesquite wood pellet.

7. Arrange the stuffed pepper on the grill grate, stuffed side up. Cook stuffed peppers for about 40 minutes.

8. Top each stuffed pepper with parmesan cheese and cook for an additional 5 minutes or until the cheese is melted.

Nutrition:

- Carbohydrates: 32 g.
- Protein: 18 g.
- Fat: 6 g.
- Sodium: 12 mg.
- Cholesterol: 151 mg.

PORK RECIPES

22. Pork Chops

Preparation time: 35 minutes.

Cooking time: 40 minutes.

Servings: 4

Pellets: apple.

Ingredients:

- ✓ 8 oz. pork chops.
- ✓ Salt and pepper.
- ✓ 1/4 cup apple cider.
- ✓ 2 cinnamon sticks.
- ✓ 12 peppercorns.
- ✓ 6 cloves garlic, minced.
- ✓ 1-inch fresh ginger, minced.
- ✓ 3 tbsp. butter.
- ✓ 3 tbsp. shallot, minced.
- ✓ 3 cup apples and pears, chopped.
- ✓ 1/2 tsp. cinnamon.
- ✓ 1/4 tsp. nutmeg.
- ✓ 2 tsp. thyme leaves.
- ✓ 1/2 cup chicken stock.
- ✓ 2 tbsp. Dijon mustard.
- ✓ 2 tbsp. olive oil.

Preparation:

1. In a saucepan, mix the salt in warm water until it dissolves before adding the ginger and cinnamon. Let it cool, add the pork chops, and store in the refrigerator for 24 hours.

2. Take the pork out and pat them dry.

3. In a pan, warm up the butter and add the shallots, pears, apples, nutmeg, and thyme, and cook for 8 minutes.

4. Next, increase the heat and add the apple cider and chicken stock and cook for a further 5 minutes.

5. Take off the heat and mix in the mustard.

6. When ready to cook, set the smoker to 500° F and preheat.

7. Brush the pork chops with olive oil and put them straight on the grill, and cook for 7 minutes.

8. Turn the chops and cook for 10 more minutes.

9. Remove from the grill and serve with your fruit mixture.

Nutrition:

- Carbohydrates: 56 g.

- Protein: 34 g.

- Fat: 54 g.

- Sodium: 11 mg.

- Cholesterol: 123 mg.

23. BBQ Pulled Pork

Preparation time: 15 minutes.

Cooking time: 10 hours.

Servings: 6

Pellets: cherry.

Ingredients:

- ✓ 1 tbsp. red hot sauce.
- ✓ Salt and pepper.
- ✓ 1 tsp. mustard powder.
- ✓ 1 tsp. garlic powder.
- ✓ 2 cups apple cider vinegar.
- ✓ 1 tsp. red pepper flakes.
- ✓ 6 tbsp. paprika.
- ✓ 1 tsp. cinnamon.
- ✓ 1 tsp. ground sage.
- ✓ 4 tbsp. honey.
- ✓ 6 lbs. pork butt.
- ✓ 1 cup pork rub.
- ✓ 1/2 cup unsweetened apple juice.

Preparation:

1. Begin by setting your smoker temperature to 225° F and preheat.

2. Mix the red hot sauce, mustard powder, garlic powder, red pepper flakes, paprika, cinnamon, ground sage, and honey together and set to 1 side.

3. Season your pork with the rub, and leave to rest for 20 minutes.

4. Put the pork straight on the grill and cook for 5 hours.

5. Wrap the pork in foil and pour apple juice into the foil, then get it back on the grill.

6. Up the smoker temperature to 250° F and cook for 3 more hours.

7. To serve, shred the pork and drizzle with the sauce.

Nutrition:

- Carbohydrates: 32 g.
- Protein: 18 g.
- Fat: 6 g.
- Sodium: 12 mg.
- Cholesterol: 151 mg.

24. Pork Broil

Preparation time: 30 minutes.

Cooking time: 1 hour.

Servings: 8

Pellets: pecan.

Ingredients:

- ✓ 2 tbsp. olive oil.
- ✓ 2 lbs. potatoes.
- ✓ 6 corn ears.
- ✓ 2 lbs. smoked kielbasa sausage.
- ✓ 3 lbs. shrimp, deveined.
- ✓ 2 tbsp. butter.

Preparation:

1. When ready, turn the smoker to 450° F and preheat for 15 minutes.

2. Coat your potatoes with olive oil and season. Put straight onto the grill and roast for 20 minutes.

3. Use the remaining oil to drizzle your corn and place along with the sausage on the grill, roasting for a further 15 minutes.

4. Add the shrimp and grill for 10 more minutes.

5. Smother in melted butter and serve.

Nutrition:

- Calories: 122.

- Fat: 3 g.

- Sodium: 48 mg.

- Carbohydrates: 0 g.

- Fiber: 0 g.

- Sugars: 0 g.

- Protein: 22 g.

25. Smoked Pork Chops

Preparation time: 5 minutes.

Cooking time: 1 hour.

Servings: 4

Pellets: cherry.

Ingredients:

- ✓ 8 oz. pork rib chops.
- ✓ Poultry rub.
- ✓ 1 cup ginger ale.
- ✓ 1/4 cup brown sugar.
- ✓ 1/2 cup balsamic vinegar.
- ✓ 2 sprigs rosemary.
- ✓ Olive oil as needed.

Preparation:

1. Start by setting the smoker temperature to 165° F and preheat.

2. Use the poultry rub to season the chops gently and thoroughly.

3. Put the chops on the grill and smoke for 30 minutes.

4. In the meantime, reduce brown sugar, ginger ale, vinegar, and rosemary on a low heat until it thickens. This should take about 20 minutes.

5. Take the chops off the grill and increase the temperature to 500° F.

6. Drizzle the pork chops with oil and place them back on the grill for 5 minutes.

7. Turn the chops and cover in the glaze, cook for a further 5 minutes, slice, and serve.

Nutrition:

- Carbohydrates: 67 g.

- Protein: 13 g.

- Fat: 10 g.

- Sodium: 18 mg.

- Cholesterol: 145 mg.

26. Pineapple Pork Chops

Preparation time: 30 minutes.

Cooking time: 20 minutes.

Servings: 4

Pellets: apple.

Ingredients:

- ✓ 16 lbs. pork chops.
- ✓ 2 tbsp. poultry rub.
- ✓ 1 mango, cubed.
- ✓ 1/2 pineapple, chopped.
- ✓ 1 red bell pepper, chopped.
- ✓ 1 jalapeño, seeded and diced.
- ✓ 1/2 red onion, diced.
- ✓ 2 tbsp. cilantro, diced.
- ✓ 1 lime, juiced.
- ✓ 1 clove garlic, minced.
- ✓ Salt and pepper.
- ✓ 1/4 cup BBQ sauce.

Preparation:

1. Smear the pork chops with the rub and leave them in the refrigerator for 30 minutes.

2. To make the salsa, mix the mango, pineapple, red bell pepper, jalapeño, red onion, cilantro, lime, garlic, salt, and pepper, in a bowl and leave to 1 side.

3. Next, set the temperature to 500° F and preheat.

4. Grill the chops for 7 minutes, turning and brushing with the BBQ sauce, then cooking for 7 more minutes.

5. Serve with salsa. Enjoy!

Nutrition:

- Carbohydrates: 56 g.

- Protein: 12 g.

- Fat: 26 g.

- Sodium: 23 mg.

- Cholesterol: 16 mg.

27. Pulled Pork Sandwich

Preparation time: 30 minutes.

Cooking time: 1 hour.

Servings: 4

Pellets: apple.

Ingredients:

- ✓ 4 oranges, juiced.
- ✓ 4 limes, juiced.
- ✓ 3 tbsp. brown sugar.
- ✓ 4 tbsp. chili powder.
- ✓ Salt and pepper.
- ✓ 8 oz. cooked pulled pork.
- ✓ 1 loaf bread.
- ✓ Butter as needed.
- ✓ Mustard as needed.
- ✓ 4 slices cheese.

Preparation:

1. In a saucepan on high heat, warm the lime juice, orange juice, sugar, chili powder, salt, and pepper, until they have dissolved.

2. Stir in the pork and set your smoker to 500° F, and preheat.

3. Heat 2 pans on the grill and start making your sandwich.

4. Slice the bread and spread butter on each side. Spread mustard on 1 side and add the cheese slides, then add the cooked pork.

5. Place on the grill for 5 minutes, then remove and serve.

Nutrition:

- Carbohydrates: 67 g.

- Protein: 13 g.

- Fat: 16 g.

- Sodium: 23 mg.

- Cholesterol: 12 mg.

28. Rack of Ribs

Preparation time: 15 minutes.

Cooking time: 6 hours.

Servings: 6

Pellets: hickory.

Ingredients:

- ✓ 2 racks baby back pork ribs.
- ✓ 1/3 cup mustard.
- ✓ 1/2 cup apple juice.
- ✓ 1 tbsp. Worcestershire sauce.
- ✓ Poultry rub.
- ✓ 1/2 cup brown sugar.
- ✓ 1/3 cup honey.
- ✓ 1 cup BBQ sauce.

Preparation:

1. In a bowl, mix together the mustard, half of the apple juice, and Worcestershire sauce. Spread the mixture over your ribs and rub with the poultry rub.

2. Set your smoker's temperature to 180° F and preheat for 15 minutes. Smoke the ribs for 3 hours, then change the grill temperature to 225° F.

3. Cover the ribs in foil and sprinkle with sugar, honey, and the remaining apple juice.

4. Return the covered ribs to the grill for 2 more hours, then remove the foil, and grill for another hour.

5. Smear with the BBQ sauce and serve.

Nutrition:

- Carbohydrates: 12 g.
- Protein: 28 g.
- Fat: 16 g.
- Sodium: 23 mg.
- Cholesterol: 21 mg.

29. Pork Tenderloin

Preparation time: 5 minutes.

Cooking time: 3 hours.

Servings: 4

Pellets: apple.

Ingredients:

- ✓ 3 tbsp. honey.
- ✓ 1/4 cup brown sugar.
- ✓ 2 tbsp. thyme leaves.
- ✓ 3 tbsp. poultry rub.
- ✓ 1/2 cup apple juice.
- ✓ Salt and pepper.
- ✓ 2 lb. pork tenderloins.

Preparation:

1. In a big bowl, mix the honey, apple juice, rub, sugar, black pepper, and thyme.

2. Add the pork to the bowl and spread the mix over it, then cover it in plastic before putting it in the refrigerator for 3 hours.

3. Set your smoker to 225° F and preheat.

4. Grill the pork for 3 hours before slicing and serving.

Nutrition:

- Carbohydrates: 45 g.

- Protein: 23 g.

- Fat: 18 g.

- Sodium: 45 mg.

- Cholesterol: 12 mg.

30. BBQ Pork Ribs

Preparation time: 30 minutes.

Cooking time: 5 hours.

Servings: 6

Pellets: cherry.

Ingredients:

- ✓ 2 racks pork ribs.
- ✓ 1 cup poultry rub.
- ✓ 1/8 cup brown sugar.
- ✓ 4 tbsp. butter.
- ✓ 4 tbsp. agave.
- ✓ 1 bottle BBQ sauce.

Preparation:

1. Start by turning your smoker to 225° F and preheat.
2. Season the ribs with the rub and leave to rest for 20 minutes.
3. Put the ribs on the grill and cook for 3 hours.
4. Spread half of the brown sugar, the butter, and the agave onto a large piece of foil.
5. Place the cooked ribs onto the foil, place the second half of the brown sugar, butter, and agave onto the

other side of the ribs. Wrap the ribs in the foil, then turn your grill up to 250° F, and put the wrapped ribs back on the smoker.

6. Cook for a further 2 hours before removing the foil and cooking for a final 10 minutes.

7. Remove and serve with the BBQ sauce.

Nutrition:

- Carbohydrates: 3 g.

- Protein: 15 g.

- Fat: 16 g.

- Sodium: 23 mg.

- Cholesterol: 23 mg.

31. Pork Chili Verde

Preparation time: 20 minutes.

Cooking time: 2 hours.

Servings: 6

Pellets: hickory.

Ingredients:

- ✓ 3 lbs. pork shoulder.
- ✓ 1 tbsp. all-purpose flour.
- ✓ Salt and pepper.
- ✓ 1 lb. tomatillos.
- ✓ 2 jalapeños, seeded.
- ✓ 1 onion, cut into wedges.
- ✓ 4 cloves garlic.
- ✓ 4 tbsp. olive oil.
- ✓ 2 cups chicken stock.
- ✓ 2 cans green chilies.
- ✓ 1 tbsp. oregano.
- ✓ 1 tbsp. cumin.
- ✓ 1/2 lime, for serving.
- ✓ 1/4 cup cilantro, for serving.

Preparation:

1. Place pork shoulder in a medium bowl, coat with flour, and season with salt and pepper.

2. Once you are ready to cook, set the smoker's temperature to 500° F before closing the lid and leaving it to preheat for at least 15 minutes.

3. Next, lay a sizable cast iron pan straight onto the lowest rack of your grill, and leave it to preheat for no less than 20 minutes.

4. Next, lay the jalapeños, garlic, tomatillos, and onion onto a sheet tray, which should be lined with a layer of parchment paper. Then, drizzle the vegetables with olive oil before seasoning with further salt and pepper. Stir thoroughly to make sure they are well coated and even.

5. Pour the final 2 tbsp. of oil into the cast iron skillet on the bottom rack of the smoker before adding the pork shoulder, making sure that the meat is evenly distributed across the pan.

6. Lay the sheet tray with vegetables onto the rack at the top of the smoker before closing the lid. Leave both the vegetables and pork to cook for 20 minutes without checking it or opening up the lid. This should allow the pork to brown on the bottom and let the vegetables begin to soften.

7. Once the 20 minutes is up, take the vegetables off of the grill, before transferring them from the tray

and into the blender. Puree the vegetables until they create a smooth mixture.

8. Pour out the vegetables into a fresh, larger pan, along with the pork, the oregano, the cumin, the chilies, and the chicken stock.

9. Shut the lid of your smoker and lower the temperature down to 325° F. Cook the mix for a further 90 minutes until there is no liquid, and the pork has become soft and tender. If the pork reduces too quickly and the pork is not tender yet, then you can add some more chicken stock as you need it until you are able to pull the pork apart using just a fork.

10. Take the mixture off of the grill and finish it off with lime juice and chopped cilantro. Serve in the way you desire, such as in a rice bowl, with tacos, or as a burrito.

Nutrition:

- Carbohydrates: 3 g.

- Protein: 12 g.

- Fat:

- Sodium:

- Cholesterol: 34 mg.

32. Smoked Sausages

Preparation time: 30 minutes.

Cooking time: 3 hours.

Servings: 4

Pellets: mesquite.

Ingredients:

- ✓ 3 lbs. ground pork.
- ✓ 1 tsp. pink curing salt.
- ✓ 1/2 cup ice water.
- ✓ 1 tbsp. onion powder.
- ✓ 1/2 tbsp. ground mustard.
- ✓ Salt and black pepper.
- ✓ 1 tbsp. garlic powder.
- ✓ Hog casings, soaked and rinsed in cold water.

Preparation:

1. Start by getting a medium-sized bowl, mixing together the seasonings and the meat, combining until they are well blended.

2. Add in some ice-cold water to the mixture and work into the mixture until everything has been successfully merged.

3. Put the mix into a sausage stuffer before using it to create a string of sausages. Be sure not to stuff them too much. Otherwise, the casing may end up bursting.

4. After you have stuffed all of the sausage meat, pinch where you want each sausage to start and end before twisting and creating links.

5. When ready to cook, set your smoker temperature to 225° F before leaving it to preheat for 15 minutes.

6. Place your sausage links on to the smoker directly before smoking for 2 hours. Remove the sausages, and let them rest for 5 minutes before you slice and serve them.

Nutrition:

- Carbohydrates: 12 g.

- Protein: 13 g.

- Fat:

- Sodium: 23 mg.

- Cholesterol: 21 mg.

LAMB RECIPES

33. Roasted Leg of Lamb

Preparation time: 30 minutes.

Cooking time: 2 hours.

Servings: 12

Ingredients:

- ✓ 8 lbs. leg of lamb, bone-in, fat trimmed.

- ✓ 2 lemons, juiced, zester.

- ✓ 1 tbsp. minced garlic.

- ✓ 4 sprigs of rosemary, 1-inch dice.

- ✓ 4 cloves of garlic, peeled, sliced lengthwise.

- ✓ Salt as needed.

- ✓ Ground black pepper as needed.

- ✓ 2 tsp. olive oil.

Preparation:

1. Switch on the pellet grill fill the grill hopper with cherry flavored wood pellets, power the grill on by using the control panel, select smoke on the temperature dial, or set the temperature to 450° F and let it preheat for a minimum of 15 minutes.

2. Meanwhile, take a small bowl, place minced garlic in it, stir in oil and then rub this mixture on all sides of the lamb leg.

3. Then make ¾-inch deep cuts into the lamb meat, about 2 dozen, stuff each cut with garlic slices and rosemary, sprinkle with lemon zest, drizzle with lemon juice, and then season well with salt and black pepper.

4. When the grill has preheated, open the lid, place the lamb's leg on the grill grate, shut the grill, and smoke for 30 minutes.

5. Change the smoking temperature to 350° F and then continue smoking for 1 hour 30 minutes until the internal temperature reaches 130° F.

6. When done, transfer lamb to a cutting board, let it rest for 15 minutes, then cut it into slices and serve.

Nutrition:

- Calories: 219.
- Fat: 14 g.
- Carbohydrates: 1 g.
- Protein: 22 g.
- Fiber: 0 g.

34. Smoked Rack of Lamb

Preparation time: 10 minutes.

Cooking time: 1 hour 15 minutes.

Servings: 4

Ingredients:

✓ 1 rack of lamb rib, membrane removed

For the marinade:

✓ 1 lemon, juiced.

✓ 2 tsp. minced garlic.

✓ 1 tsp. salt.

✓ 1 tsp. ground black pepper.

✓ 1 tsp. dried thyme.

✓ ¼ cup balsamic vinegar.

✓ 1 tsp. dried basil.

For the glaze:

- 2 tbsp. soy sauce.
- ¼ cup Dijon mustard.
- 2 tbsp. Worcestershire sauce.
- ¼ cup red wine.

Preparation:

1. Prepare the marinade and for this, take a small bowl, place all the ingredients in it and whisk until combined.

2. Place the rack of lamb into a large plastic bag, pour in marinade, seal the bag, turn it upside down to coat lamb with the marinade and let it marinate for a minimum of 8 hours in the refrigerator.

3. When ready to cook, switch on the pellet grill, fill the grill hopper with flavored wood pellets, power the grill on by using the control panel, select smoke on the temperature dial, or set the temperature to 300° F and let it preheat for a minimum of 5 minutes.

4. Meanwhile, prepare the glaze and for this, take a small bowl, place all of its ingredients in it and whisk until combined.

5. When the grill has preheated, open the lid, place lamb rack on the grill grate, shut the grill, and smoke for 15 minutes.

6. Brush with glaze, flip the lamb and then continue smoking for 1 hour 15 minutes until the internal temperature reaches 145° F, basting with the glaze every 30 minutes.

7. When done, transfer lamb rack to a cutting board, let it rest for 15 minutes, cut it into slices, and then serve.

Nutrition:

- Calories: 323.
- Fat: 18 g.
- Carbohydrates: 13 g.
- Protein: 25 g.
- Fiber: 1 g.

35. Rosemary Lamb

Preparation time: 10 minutes.

Cooking time: 3 hours.

Servings: 2

Ingredients:

- ✓ 1 rack of lamb rib, membrane removed.
- ✓ 12 baby potatoes.
- ✓ 1 bunch of asparagus, ends trimmed.
- ✓ Ground black pepper, as needed.
- ✓ Salt, as needed.
- ✓ 1 tsp. dried rosemary.
- ✓ 2 tbsp. olive oil.
- ✓ 1/2 cup butter, unsalted.

Preparation:

1. Switch on the pellet grill fill the grill hopper with flavored wood pellets, power the grill on by using the control panel, select smoke on the temperature dial, or set the temperature to 225° F and let it preheat for a minimum of 5 minutes.

2. Meanwhile, drizzle oil on both sides of lamb ribs and then sprinkle with rosemary.

3. Take a deep baking dish, place potatoes in it, add butter and mix until coated.

4. When the grill has preheated, open the lid, place lamb ribs on the grill grate along with potatoes in the baking dish, shut the grill, and smoke for 3 hours until the internal temperature reaches 145° F.

5. Add asparagus into the baking dish in the last 20 minutes and, when done, remove the baking dish from the grill and transfer lamb to a cutting board.

6. Let lamb rest for 15 minutes, cut it into slices, and then serve with potatoes and asparagus.

Nutrition:

- Calories: 355.
- Fat: 12.5 g.
- Carbohydrates: 25 g.
- Protein: 35 g.
- Fiber: 6 g.

36. Lamb Chops With Rosemary and Olive Oil

Preparation time: 10 minutes.

Cooking time: 50 minutes.

Servings: 4

Ingredients:

- 12 lamb loin chops, fat trimmed.
- 1 tbsp. chopped rosemary leaves.
- Salt as needed for dry brining.
- Jeff's original rub as needed.
- ¼ cup olive oil.

Preparation:

1. Take a cookie sheet, place lamb chops on it, sprinkle with salt, and then refrigerate for 2 hours.

2. Meanwhile, take a small bowl, place rosemary leaves in it, stir in oil and let the mixture stand for 1 hour.

3. When ready to cook, switch on the pellet grill, fill the grill hopper with apple-flavored wood pellets,

111

power the grill on by using the control panel, select smoke on the temperature dial, or set the temperature to 225° F and let it preheat for a minimum of 5 minutes.

4. Meanwhile, brush rosemary-oil mixture on all sides of lamb chops and then sprinkle with Jeff's original rub.

5. When the grill has preheated, open the lid, place lamb chops on the grill grate, shut the grill, and smoke for 50 minutes until the lamb chops' internal temperature reaches 138° F.

6. When done, wrap lamb chops in foil, let them rest for 7 minutes and then serve.

Nutrition:

*   Calories: 171.5.

*   Fat: 7.8 g.

*   Carbohydrates: 0.4 g.

*   Protein: 23.2 g.

*   Fiber: 0.1 g.

37. Boneless Leg of Lamb

Preparation time: 10 minutes.

Cooking time: 4 hours.

Servings: 4

Ingredients:

✓ 2 1/2 lbs. leg of lamb, boneless, fat trimmed.

For the marinade:

✓ 2 tsp. minced garlic.

✓ 1 tbsp. ground black pepper.

✓ 2 tbsp. salt.

✓ 1 tsp. thyme.

✓ 2 tbsp. oregano.

✓ 2 tbsp. olive oil.

Preparation:

1. Take a small bowl, place all the ingredients for the marinade in it and then stir until combined.

2. Rub the marinade on all sides of lamb, then place it in a large sheet, cover with a plastic wrap and marinate for a minimum of 1 hour in the refrigerator.

3. When ready to cook, switch on the pellet grill, fill the grill hopper with apple-flavored wood pellets, power the grill on by using the control panel, select "smoke" on the temperature dial, or set the temperature to 250° F and let it preheat for a minimum of 5 minutes.

4. Meanwhile, when the grill has preheated, open the lid, place the lamb on the grill grate, shut the grill, and smoke for 4 hours until the internal temperature reaches 145° F.

5. When done, transfer lamb to a cutting board, let it stand for 10 minutes, then carve it into slices and serve.

Nutrition:

- Calories: 213.
- Fat: 9 g.
- Carbohydrates: 1 g.
- Protein: 29 g.
- Fiber: 0 g.

38. Smoked Lamb Shoulder

Preparation time: 10 minutes.

Cooking time: 4 hours.

Servings: 6

Ingredients:

- 8 lbs. lamb shoulder, fat trimmed.
- 2 tbsp. olive oil.
- Salt as needed.

For the rub:

- 1 tbsp. dried oregano.
- 2 tbsp. salt.
- 1 tbsp. crushed dried bay leaf.
- 1 tbsp. sugar.
- 2 tbsp. dried crushed sage.
- 1 tbsp. dried thyme.
- 1 tbsp. ground black pepper.
- 1 tbsp. dried basil.

- 1 tbsp. dried rosemary.

- 1 tbsp. dried parsley.

Preparation:

1. Switch on the pellet grill fill the grill hopper with cherry flavored wood pellets, power the grill on by using the control panel, select smoke on the temperature dial, or set the temperature to 250° F and let it preheat for a minimum of 5 minutes.

2. Meanwhile, prepare the rub and for this, take a small bowl, place all of its ingredients in it and stir until mixed.

3. Brush lamb with oil and then sprinkle with prepared rub until evenly coated.

4. When the grill has preheated, open the lid, place lamb should on the grill grate fat-side up, shut the grill, and smoke for 3 hours.

5. Then change the smoking temperature to 325° F and continue smoking for 1 hour until fat renders. The internal temperature reaches 195° F.

6. When done, wrap lamb should in aluminum foil and let it rest for 20 minutes.

7. Pull lamb shoulder by using 2 forks and then serve.

Nutrition:

- Calories: 300.

- Fat: 24 g.

- Carbohydrates: 0 g.

- Protein: 19 g.

- Fiber: 0 g.

39. Herby Lamb Chops

Preparation time: 10 minutes.

Cooking time: 2 hours.

Servings: 4

Ingredients:

- 8 lamb chops, each about ¾-inch thick, fat trimmed

For the marinade:

- 1 tsp. minced garlic.
- Salt as needed.
- 1 tbsp. dried rosemary.
- Ground black pepper as needed.
- ½ tbsp. dried thyme.
- 3 tbsp. balsamic vinegar.
- 1 tbsp. Dijon mustard.
- ½ cup olive oil.

Preparation:

1. Prepare the marinade and for this, take a small bowl, place all of its ingredients in it and stir until well combined.

2. Place lamb chops in a large plastic bag, pour in marinade, seal the bag, turn it upside down to coat lamb chops with the marinade and let it marinate for a minimum of 4 hours in the refrigerator.

3. When ready to cook, switch on the Pellet grill, fill the grill hopper with flavored wood pellets, power the grill on by using the control panel, select smoke on the temperature dial, or set the temperature to 450° F and let it preheat for a minimum of 5 minutes.

4. Meanwhile, remove lamb chops from the refrigerator and bring them to room temperature.

5. When the grill has preheated, open the lid, place lamb chops on the grill grate, shut the grill, and smoke for 5 minutes per side until seared.

6. When done, transfer lamb chops to a dish, let them rest for 5 minutes and then serve.

Nutrition:

- Calories: 280.

- Fat: 12.3 g.

- Carbohydrates: 8.3 g.

- Protein: 32.7 g.

- Fiber: 1.2 g.

40. Garlic Rack of Lamb

Preparation time: 10 minutes.

Cooking time: 3 hours.

Servings: 4

Ingredients:

- 1 rack of lamb, membrane removed.

For the marinade:

- 2 tsp. minced garlic.
- 1 tsp. dried basil.
- 1/3 cup cream sherry.
- 1 tsp. dried oregano.
- 1/3 cup Marsala wine.
- 1 tsp. dried rosemary.
- ½ tsp. ground black pepper.
- 1/3 cup balsamic vinegar.
- 2 tbsp. olive oil.

Preparation:

1. Prepare the marinade and for this, take a small bowl, place all of its ingredients in it and stir until well combined.

2. Place lamb rack in a large plastic bag, pour in marinade, seal the bag, turn it upside down to coat lamb with the marinade and let it marinate for a minimum of 45 minutes in the refrigerator.

3. When ready to cook, switch on the pellet grill, fill the grill hopper with flavored wood pellets, power the grill on by using the control panel, select "smoke" on the temperature dial, or set the temperature to 250° F and let it preheat for a minimum of 5 minutes.

4. Meanwhile, when the grill has preheated, open the lid, place lamb rack on the grill grate, shut the grill, and smoke for 3 hours until the internal temperature reaches 165° F.

5. When done, transfer the lamb rack to a cutting board, rest for 10 minutes, and then cut into slices and serve.

Nutrition:

- Calories: 210.
- Fat: 11 g.
- Carbohydrates: 3 g.
- Protein: 25 g.
- Fiber: 1 g.

41. Brown Sugar Lamb Chops

Preparation time: 5 minutes.

Cooking time: 10–15 minutes.

Servings: 4

Ingredients:

- ✓ Pepper.
- ✓ 1 tsp. garlic powder.
- ✓ Salt.
- ✓ 2 tsp. tarragon.
- ✓ 1 tsp. cinnamon.
- ✓ ¼ cup brown sugar.
- ✓ 4 lamb chops.
- ✓ 2 tsp. ginger.

Preparation:

1. Combine the salt, garlic powder, pepper, cinnamon, tarragon, ginger, and sugar. Coat the lamb chops in the mixture and chill for 2 hours.

2. Add wood pellets to your smoker and follow your cooker's startup procedure. Preheat your smoker, with your lid closed, until it reaches 450° F. Place the chops on the grill, cover, and smoke for 10–15 minutes per side. Serve.

Nutrition:

- Calories: 210.
- Fat: 11 g.
- Carbohydrates: 3 g.
- Protein: 25 g.
- Fiber: 1 g.

42. Aromatic Herbed Rack of Lamb

Preparation time: 10 minutes.

Cooking time: 2 hours.

Servings: 8

Ingredients:

- ✓ 2 tbsp. fresh sage.
- ✓ 2 tbsp. fresh rosemary.
- ✓ 2 tbsp. fresh thyme.
- ✓ 2 garlic cloves, peeled.
- ✓ 1 tbsp. honey.
- ✓ Salt and freshly ground black pepper, to taste.
- ✓ ¼ cup olive oil.
- ✓ 1 (1½-lb.) rack of lamb, trimmed.

Preparation:

1. In a food processor, add all ingredients except for oil and rack of lamb rack and pulse until well combined.

2. While the motor is running, slowly add oil and pulse until a smooth paste is formed.

3. Coat the rib rack with paste generously and refrigerate for about 2 hours.

4. Set the temperature of Traeger Grill to 225° F and preheat with a closed lid for 15 minutes.

5. Arrange the rack of lamb onto the grill and cook for about 2 hours.

6. Remove the rack of lamb from the grill and place onto a cutting board for about 10–15 minutes before slicing.

7. With a sharp knife, cut the rack into individual ribs and serve.

Nutrition:

- Calories: 566.

- Carbohydrates: 9.8 g.

- Protein: 46.7 g.

- Fat: 33.5 g.

- Sugar: 5.8 g.

- Sodium: 214 mg.

- Fiber: 2.2 g.

43. Leg of a Lamb

Preparation time: 15 minutes.

Cooking time: 2 hours 30 minutes.

Servings: 10

Ingredients:

- ✓ 1 (8-oz.) package softened cream cheese.

- ✓ ¼ cup cooked and crumbled bacon.

- ✓ 1 seeded and chopped jalapeño pepper.

- ✓ 1 tbsp. crushed dried rosemary.

- ✓ 2 tsp. garlic powder.

- ✓ 1 tsp. onion powder.

- ✓ 1 tsp. paprika.

- ✓ 1 tsp. cayenne pepper.

- ✓ Salt, to taste.

- ✓ 1 (4–5-lb.) butterflied leg of lamb.

- ✓ 2–3 tbsp. olive oil.

Preparation:

1. For filling in a bowl, add all ingredients and mix till well combined.

2. For spice mixture in another small bowl, mix together all ingredients.

3. Place the leg of lamb onto a smooth surface. Sprinkle the inside of the leg with some spice mixture.

4. Place filling mixture over the inside surface evenly. Roll the leg of lamb tightly and with a butcher's twine, tie the roll to secure the filling

5. Coat the outer side of the roll with olive oil evenly and then sprinkle with spice mixture.

6. Preheat the pallet grill to 225–240° F.

7. Arrange the leg of lamb in a pallet grill and cook for about 2–2½ hours. Remove the leg of lamb from the pallet grill and transfer it onto a cutting board.

8. With a piece of foil, cover leg loosely and transfer onto a cutting board for about 20–25 minutes before slicing.

9. With a sharp knife, cut the leg of lamb in desired sized slices and serve.

Nutrition:

- Calories: 715.
- Fat: 38.9 g.
- Carbohydrates: 2.2 g.
- Protein: 84.6 g.
- Fiber: 0.1 g.

BURGER RECIPE

44. Cheesy Lamb Burgers

Preparation time: 5 minutes.

Cooking time: 20 minutes.

Servings: 6

Ingredients:

- ✓ 2 lb. ground lamb.
- ✓ 1 cup Parmigiano-Reggiano cheese, grated.
- ✓ Salt and freshly ground black pepper, to taste.

Preparation:

1. Set the temperature of the Traeger grill to 425° F and preheat with a closed lid for 15 minutes.

2. In a bowl, add all ingredients and mix well.

3. Make 4 (¾-inch thick) patties from the mixture.

4. With your thumbs, make a shallow but wide depression in each patty.

5. Arrange the patties onto the grill, depression-side down, and cook for about 8 minutes.

6. Flip and cook for about 8–10 minutes.

Nutrition

- Sodium: 370 mg.
- Total carbohydrates: 12 g.
- Fiber: 8 g.

45. No-fuss Tuna Burgers

Preparation time: 3 minutes.

Cooking time: 15 minutes.

Servings: 4

Ingredients:

- ✓ 2 lb. tuna steak.
- ✓ 1 green bell pepper, seeded and chopped.
- ✓ 1 white onion, chopped.
- ✓ 2 eggs.
- ✓ 1 tsp. soy sauce.
- ✓ 1 tbsp. blackened Saskatchewan rub.
- ✓ Salt and freshly ground black pepper, to taste.

Preparation:

1. Set the temperature of the Traeger grill to 500° F and preheat with a closed lid for 15 minutes.

2. In a bowl, add all the ingredients and mix until well combined.

3. With greased hands, make patties from the mixture.

4. Place the patties onto the grill close to the edges and cook for about 10–15 minutes, flipping once halfway through.

5. Serve hot.

Nutrition:

- Calories: 313.

- Carbohydrates: 3.4 g.

- Protein: 47.5 g.

- Fat: 11 g.

- Sugar: 1.9 g.

- Sodium: 174 mg.

- Fiber: 0.7 g.

46. Apple Veggie Burger

Preparation time: 5 minutes.

Cooking time: 35 minutes.

Servings: 6

Ingredients:

- ✓ 3 tbsp. ground flax or ground chia.
- ✓ 1/3 cup of warm water.
- ✓ 1/2 cup rolled oats.
- ✓ 1 cup chickpeas, drained and rinsed.
- ✓ 1 tsp. cumin.
- ✓ 1/2 cup onion.
- ✓ 1 tsp. dried basil.

- ✓ 2 Granny Smith apples.
- ✓ 1/3 cup parsley or cilantro, chopped.
- ✓ 2 tbsp. soy sauce.
- ✓ 2 tsp. liquid smoke.
- ✓ 2 cloves garlic, minced.
- ✓ 1 tsp. chili powder.
- ✓ 1/4 tsp. black pepper.

Preparation:

1. Preheat the smoker to 225° F while adding wood chips and water to it.

2. In a separate bowl, add chickpeas and mash. Mix the remaining ingredients along with the dipped flax seeds.

3. Form patties from this mixture.

4. Put the patties on the rack of the smoker and smoke them for 20 minutes on each side.

5. When brown, take them out and serve.

Nutrition:

- Calories: 24.

- Cal fat: 5 g.

- Carbohydrates: 40 g.

- Protein: 9 g.

- Fiber: 10.3 g.

47. Chili Cheeseburgers

Preparation time: 4 minutes.

Cooking time: 30 minutes.

Servings: 6

Ingredients:

- ✓ 1 lb. ground chuck (80% lean, 20% fat).
- ✓ 4 Monterey Jack cheese slices.
- ✓ 1/4 cup yellow onion, finely chopped.
- ✓ 4 hamburger buns.
- ✓ 2 tbsp. hatch chili, peeled and chopped.
- ✓ 6 tbsp. hatch chili salsa.
- ✓ 1 tsp. kosher salt.
- ✓ Mayonnaise, to taste.
- ✓ 1 tsp. ground black pepper.

Preparation:

1. In a bowl, combine beef, diced onion, chopped hatch chills, salt, and fresh ground pepper. Once evenly mixed, shape into 4 burger patties

2. Preheat pellet grill to 350° F. Place burgers on the grill, and cook for about 6 minutes per side or until both sides of each burger are slightly crispy

3. After the burger is cooked to the desired doneness and both sides have a light sear, place cheese slices on each burger. Allow to heat for around 45 seconds or until cheese melts

4. Remove from grill and allow to rest for about 10 minutes. Spread a little bit of mayonnaise on both sides of each bun. Place burger patty on the bottom side of the bun, then top with hatch chili salsa on top to taste

Nutrition:

- Calories: 228.

- Carbohydrates: 25.9 g.

- Protein: 10.6 g.

- Fat: 13.5 g.

- Sugar: 11.6 g.

- Sodium: 134 mg.

- Fiber: 9.3 g.

48. Veggie Lover's Burgers

Preparation time: 5 minutes.

Cooking time: 51 minutes.

Servings: 4

Ingredients:

- ✓ ¾ cup lentils.
- ✓ 1 tbsp. ground flaxseed.
- ✓ 2 tbsp. extra-virgin olive oil.
- ✓ 1 onion, chopped.
- ✓ 2 garlic cloves, minced.
- ✓ Salt and freshly ground black pepper, to taste.
- ✓ 1 cup walnuts, toasted.
- ✓ ¾ cup breadcrumbs.
- ✓ 1 tsp. ground cumin.
- ✓ 1 tsp. paprika.

Preparation:

1. In a pan of boiling water, add the lentils and cook for about 15 minutes or until soft.

2. Drain the lentils completely and set them aside.

3. In a small bowl, mix together the flaxseed with 4 tbsp. of water. Set aside for about 5 minutes.

4. In a medium skillet, heat the oil over medium heat and sauté the onion for about 4–6 minutes.

5. Add the garlic and a pinch of salt and pepper and sauté for about 30 seconds.

6. Remove from the heat and place the onion mixture into a food processor.

7. Add the ¾ of the lentils, flaxseed mixture, walnuts, breadcrumbs, and spices and pulse until smooth.

8. Transfer the mixture into a bowl and gently, fold in the remaining lentils.

9. Make 6 patties from the mixture.

10. Place the patties onto a parchment paper-lined plate and refrigerate for at least 30 minutes.

11. Set the temperature of Traeger grill to 425° F and preheat with closed lid for 15 minutes, using charcoal.

12. Place the burgers onto the grill and cook for about 8–10 minutes flipping once halfway through.

13. Serve hot.

Nutrition:

- Calories: 320.
- Carbohydrates: 19.9 g.
- Protein: 5.6 g.
- Fat: 18.5 g.

- Sugar: 13.6 g.

- Sodium: 130 mg.

- Fiber: 4.3 g.

49. Ranch Burgers

Preparation time: 10 minutes.

Cooking time: 30 minutes.

Serving: 4

Ingredients:

- ✓ 1 lb. ground beef (preferably 80% lean 20% fat ground chuck).
- ✓ 1/2 yellow onion, chopped.
- ✓ 1 package ranch dressing mix (1 oz.)
- ✓ 1 cup cheddar cheese, shredded.
- ✓ 1 egg, beaten.
- ✓ 4 buns, toasted (optional).
- ✓ 3/4 cup bread crumbs.
- ✓ 3/4 cup mayonnaise.
- ✓ 1/4 cup relish.
- ✓ 1/4 cup ketchup.
- ✓ 2 tbsp. Worcestershire sauce.

Preparation:

1. Mix ground beef, cheese, ranch dressing mix, egg, bread crumbs, and onion in a bowl until evenly combined.

2. Form burger mixture into 1/4 lb. circular patties.

3. Preheat pellet grill to 350° F.

4. Lightly oil grill grate and place burger patties on the grill.

5. Cook burgers until they reach an internal temperature of 155° F (typically cooks for about 6 minutes per side).

6. Remove burgers once done and let rest at room temperature for 15 minutes.

7. Combine sauce ingredients in a bowl and whisk well.

8. Place burger patties on buns and top with desired toppings, including homemade sauce.

Nutrition:

- Calories: 309.

- Carbohydrates: 26.9 g.

- Protein: 11.6 g.

- Fat: 20.5 g.

- Sugar: 13.6 g.

- Sodium: 167 g.

- Fiber: 10.3 g.

50. Grilled Tuna Burger With Ginger Mayonnaise

Preparation time: 10 minutes.

Cooking time: 20 minutes.

Servings: 4

Ingredients:

- ✓ 1 tbsp. of sesame oil, optional.
- ✓ 4 tbsp. of ginger, optional.
- ✓ 4 hamburger buns.
- ✓ Black pepper, freshly ground.
- ✓ 2 tbsp. and 1 tsp. of soy sauce.
- ✓ 4 of 5 oz. of tuna steak.
- ✓ Natural oil.
- ✓ 1/2 cup of mayonnaise.

Preparation:

1. Set the grill for direct cooking at 300° F. Use maple pellets for a robust woody taste.

2. Rub soy sauce on the tuna steak and season with pepper.

3. In another bowl, prepare a rub by mixing the ginger, mayonnaise, 1 tsp. of soy sauce, and sesame oil.

4. With a brush, apply the rub on the tuna steak then grill for 10 minutes before flipping. Grill the other side for another 10 minutes.

5. Serve immediately with fish between buns. Add mayonnaise and ginger as layers.

Nutrition:

- Calories: 220

- Protein: 21.5 g.

- Fat: 16 g.

- Carbohydrates: 23 g.

51. Lamb Burger Spiced With Curry

Preparation time: 5 minutes.

Cooking time: 20 minutes.

Servings: 4

Ingredients:

- ✓ 1/2 tsp. of turmeric.
- ✓ 1 tsp. of ground coriander.
- ✓ 1 fresh chili should be seeded and minced, preferably jalapeños chili.
- ✓ 1 tsp. of ground cumin.
- ✓ 1–1/2 lb. of boneless lamb, preferably shoulder.
- ✓ Salt and black pepper, shredded carrot.
- ✓ Red onion with scallion.
- ✓ Red bell pepper.
- ✓ Diced mango.

Preparation:

1. Set the grill for direct cooking at 300° F. Use maple pellets for a spicy, smoky taste.

2. Pulse the lamb and onions in a food processor and obtain a coarse texture.

3. Add the cumin, jalapeños chili, pepper, coriander, salt, and turmeric to a bowl. Mix thoroughly, then add the blended lamb. Stir gently.

4. Form 4 patties with the lamb mixture.

5. Grill lamb patties for 10 minutes, then flip and grill the other side for another 10 minutes

6. Serve immediately with mango, onion, and shredded carrot.

Nutrition:

- Calories: 200

- Protein: 19 g.

- Fat: 15.5 g.

- Carbohydrates: 0 g.

52. Traeger Stuffed Burgers

Preparation time: 4 minutes.

Cooking time: 15 minutes.

Servings: 6

Ingredients:

- ✓ 3 lb. ground beef.
- ✓ 1/2 tbsp. onion powder.
- ✓ 1/4 tbsp. garlic powder.
- ✓ 1 tbsp. salt.
- ✓ 1/2 tbsp. pepper.
- ✓ 1-1/2 cups Colby jack cheese, shredded.
- ✓ Johnny's seasoning salt.
- ✓ 6 slices Colby Jack cheese.

Preparation:

1. Preheat your Traeger to 375° F.

2. Mix beef, onion powder, garlic powder, salt, and pepper until well combined. Make 12 patties.

3. Place cheese on the burger patty and cover with another patty then seal the edges.

4. Season with salt, then place the patties on the grill. Cook the patties on the grill grate for 8 minutes, flip the patties and cook for additional 5 minutes.

5. Place a slice of cheese on each patty and grill with the lid closed to melt the cheese.

6. Remove the patties from the Traeger and let rest for 10 minutes. Serve and enjoy with a toasted bun.

Nutrition:

- Calories: 463.
- Total fat: 29 g.
- Saturated fat: 18 g.
- Total carbohydrates: 1 g.
- Protein: 67 g.
- Sugars 2 g.
- Fiber 0 g.
- Sodium: 590 mg.

53. Pork and Portobello Burgers

Preparation time: 5 minutes.

Cooking time: 30 minutes.

Servings: 4

Ingredients:

- ✓ 1 lb. ground pork.

- ✓ 1 tbsp. minced garlic.

- ✓ 1 tsp. minced fresh rosemary, fennel seed, or parsley.

- ✓ Salt and ground black pepper.

- ✓ 4 large Portobello mushroom caps, stems removed.

- ✓ Olive oil.

- ✓ 4 burger buns.

- ✓ Any burger fixings you like.

Preparation:

1. Combine the ground pork, garlic, rosemary, and a sprinkle of salt and pepper. Use a spoon to lightly scrape away the gills of the mushrooms and hollow them slightly. Drizzle the mushrooms (inside and out) with olive oil and sprinkle with salt and pepper. Press 1/4 of the mixture into each of the hollow sides of the mushrooms; you want the meat to spread all the way

across the width of the mushrooms. They should look like burgers.

2. Grill the burgers, meat side down, until the pork is well browned, 4–6 minutes. Flip and cook until the top side of the mushrooms are browned and the mushrooms are tender, another 6–8 minutes. If you like, use an instant-read thermometer to check the interior temperature of the pork, which should be a minimum of 145.

3. Serve the burgers on buns (toasted, if you like) with any fixings you like.

Nutrition:

- Calories: 523.7

- Fats: 43.3 g.

- Carbohydrates: 6.2 g.

- Protein: 27.3 g.

54. Grilled Chili Burger

Preparation time: 5 minutes.

Cooking time: 20 minutes.

Servings: 8

Ingredients:

- ✓ 1 tsp. of chili powder.
- ✓ 4 tsp. of butter.
- ✓ 2 lbs. of round steak, twice-grounded.
- ✓ 1 clove of garlic.
- ✓ Salt and ground pepper, preferably freshly ground.
- ✓ 1/4 cup of bread crumbs.

Preparation:

1. Set the grill for direct cooking at 300° F. Use maple pellets for a robust and woody taste.

2. Pour the meat inside a bowl and add the rest of the ingredients. Mix until well-combined. Mold the meat mixture to form 8 patties.

3. Arrange patties on the preheated cooking grid and grill for 10 minutes before flipping and grilling the other side for another 10 minutes.

4. Serve immediately with hamburger buns.

Nutrition:

- Calories: 260
- Protein: 13 g.
- Fat: 10.5 g.
- Carbohydrates: 29.9 g.

55. Grilled Lamb Burgers

Preparation time: 5 minutes.

Cooking time: 15 minutes.

Servings: 5

Ingredients:

- ✓ 1 1/4 lbs. of ground lamb.
- ✓ 1 egg.
- ✓ 1 tsp. of dried oregano.
- ✓ 1 tsp. of dry sherry.
- ✓ 1 tsp. of white wine vinegar.
- ✓ 4 minced cloves of garlic.
- ✓ Red pepper
- ✓ 1/2 cup of chopped green onions.
- ✓ 1 tbsp. of chopped mint.
- ✓ 2 tbsp. of chopped cilantro.
- ✓ 2 tbsp. of dry bread crumbs.
- ✓ 1/8 tsp. of salt to taste.
- ✓ 1/4 tsp. of ground black pepper to taste.
- ✓ 5 hamburger buns.

Preparation:

1. Preheat a wood pellet smoker or grill to 350–450° F then grease its grates. Using a large mixing bowl, add in all the ingredients on the list aside from the buns then mix properly to combine with clean hands. Make about 5 patties out of the mixture then set aside.

2. Place the lamb patties on the preheated grill and cook for about 7 to 9 minutes turning only once until an inserted thermometer reads 160° F. Serve the lamb burgers on the hamburger, add your favorite toppings and enjoy.

Nutrition:

- Calories: 376.
- Fat: 18.5 g.
- Carbohydrates: 25.4 g.
- Protein: 25.5 g.
- Fiber: 1.6 g.

POULTRY
RECIPES

56. Lemon Garlic Smoked Chicken

Preparation time: 5 minutes.

Cooking time: 3 hours 10 minutes.

Servings: 4

Ingredients:

- ✓ Whole chicken (3-lbs., 1.4-kg.)
- ✓ ½ cup the brine salt.
- ✓ 1 cup brown sugar.
- ✓ 3 ½ liters water.
- ✓ ¼ cup rub minced garlic.
- ✓ 2 tbsp. garlic powder.

- ✓ 3 tbsp. lemon juice.
- ✓ 2 ½ tbsp. paprika.
- ✓ 2 tbsp. chili powder.
- ✓ ¾ tbsp. thyme.
- ✓ 2 tbsp. cayenne.
- ✓ 1 tbsp. salt.
- ✓ 2 tbsp. black pepper.

For the filling:

- ✓ 1 cup chopped onion.
- ✓ 5 cloves garlic.
- ✓ 5 sprigs thyme.

For the heat:

✓ Mesquite wood pellets.

Preparation:

1. Stir in salt and brown sugar to the water then mix until completely dissolved. Put the chicken in the brine then soak overnight. Store in the fridge to keep it fresh. On the next day, remove the chicken from the fridge then wash and pat it dry.

2. Set aside. Combine the rub ingredients- minced garlic, garlic powder, lemon juice, paprika, chili powder, thyme, cayenne, salt, and black pepper in a bowl then mix well.

3. Rub the chicken with the spice mixture then fill the cavity with chopped onion, garlic, and thyme. Next, plug the wood pellet smoker and place the wood pellet inside the hopper.

4. Turn the switch on. Set the smoke setting and prepare the wood pellet smoker for indirect heat. Adjust the temperature to 225° F (107° C) and place the seasoned whole chicken in the wood pellet smoker. Smoke the chicken for approximately 3 hours or until the internal temperature has reached 165° F (74° C). Once it is done, remove the smoked chicken from the wood pellet smoker and let it sit for about 10 minutes.

5. Place the smoked chicken on a serving dish then serve.

Nutrition:

- Calories: 141.3.

- Fat: 1.5 g.

- Carbohydrates: 3 g.

- Protein: 27 g.

57. Sweet Honey Smoked Brown Turkey

Preparation time: 15 minutes.

Cooking time: 4 hours 40 minutes.

Servings: 4

Ingredients:

- ✓ Whole turkey (6-lbs., 2.7-kg.)
- ✓ 5 tbsp. rub salt.
- ✓ 5 tbsp. brown sugar.
- ✓ 1 tbsp. thyme.
- ✓ 1 tbsp. chopped rosemary.
- ✓ 1 tbsp. sage.
- ✓ 2 ½ tsp. black pepper.
- ✓ 2 tsp. garlic powder.
- ✓ 1 cup glaze raw honey.
- ✓ 3 tbsp. brown sugar.
- ✓ 2 tbsp. apple cider vinegar.
- ✓ ¾ tbsp. mustard.
- ✓ 1 tsp. salt.
- ✓ 2 tsp. pepper.

For the heat:

- ✓ Maple wood pellets.

Preparation:

1. Combine the salt, brown sugar, thyme, chopped parsley, and sage, black pepper, and garlic powder in a bowl then mix well. Rub the turkey with the spice mixture then let it rest for a few minutes.

2. Next, plug the wood pellet smoker and place the wood pellet inside the hopper. Turn the switch on. Set the smoke setting and prepare the wood pellet smoker for indirect heat. Adjust the temperature to 375° F (191° C) and place the seasoned turkey in the wood pellet smoker. Smoke the turkey for approximately 20 minutes or until the skin of the turkey turns brown.

3. After that, reduce the temperature to 325° F (163° C) and continue smoking the turkey for approximately 4 hours or until the internal temperature has reached 165° F (74° C). Quickly place brown sugar, apple cider vinegar, mustard, salt, and pepper in a bowl then pour raw honey over the mixture. Stir until combined.

4. Baste the smoked turkey with the honey mixture then return it back to the wood pellet smoker. Smoke the turkey for another 20 minutes then remove from the wood pellet smoker. Let the smoked turkey rest for a few minutes then cut into small pieces.

5. Serve and enjoy!

Nutrition:

- Calories: 178.
- Carbohydrates: 0 g.
- Fat: 15 g.
- Protein: 28 g.

58. Spicy Smoked Chicken Garlic

Preparation time: 10 minutes.

Cooking time: 3 hours 10 minutes.

Servings: 4

Ingredients:

- ✓ Whole chicken (3-lbs., 1.4-kg.)
- ✓ 1 tsp. rub salt.
- ✓ 1 tsp. paprika.
- ✓ 1 ½ garlic powder.
- ✓ 1 ½ black pepper.
- ✓ 2 tsp. red chili flakes.
- ✓ ½ tsp. cayenne pepper.
- ✓ ¾ tsp. thyme.
- ✓ ½ oregano.
- ✓ 3 tbsp. brown sugar.

For the heat:

- ✓ Apple wood pellets.

Preparation:

1. Rub the chicken with salt, paprika, garlic powder, black pepper, red chili flakes, cayenne pepper, thyme, oregano, and brown sugar. Wrap the seasoned chicken with plastic wrap then let it rest

for approximately an hour. Store in the fridge to keep it fresh.

2. Plug the wood pellet smoker and place the wood pellet inside the hopper. Turn the switch on. Set the smoke setting and prepare the wood pellet smoker for indirect heat. Take the chicken out of the fridge and thaw at room temperature.

3. Discard the plastic wrap. Once the wood pellet smoker is ready, place the seasoned chicken in the wood pellet smoker and smoke for approximately 10 minutes.

4. Adjust the temperature to 225° F (107° C) and continue smoking the chicken for approximately 3 hours or until the internal temperature has reached 165° F (74° C).

5. Once it is done, remove the smoked chicken from the wood pellet smoker and place it on a serving dish. Cut the smoked chicken into pieces then serve.

6. Enjoy!

Nutrition:

- Calories: 179.

- Carbohydrates: 0 g.

- Fat: 13 g.

- Protein: 42 g.

59. Hot Smoked Shredded Chicken With Sweet Sticky Sauce

Preparation time: 10 minutes.

Cooking time: 3 hours 10 minutes.

Servings: 4

Ingredients:

- ✓ Boneless chicken breast (3-lbs., 1.4-kg.)
- ✓ 3 tbsp. rub paprika.
- ✓ 3 tbsp. chili powder.
- ✓ 1 ½ tbsp. thyme.
- ✓ 1 ½ tbsp. garlic powder.
- ✓ 1 ½ tbsp. onion powder.
- ✓ 3 tbsp. cayenne.
- ✓ 1 ½ tbsp. salt.
- ✓ 1 ½ tbsp. black pepper.

For the sauce honey:

- ✓ ¼ cup maple syrup.
- ✓ 2 tbsp. brown sugar.

For the heat:

✓ Maple wood pellets.

Preparation:

1. Combine the rub ingredients — paprika, chili powder, thyme, garlic powder, onion powder, cayenne, salt, and black pepper in a bowl then mix well. Score the chicken breast and rub with the spice mixture. Let it rest for a few minutes.

2. Next, plug the wood pellet smoker and place the wood pellet inside the hopper. Turn the switch on. Set the smoke setting and prepare the wood pellet smoker for indirect heat.

3. Once the wood pellet smoker is ready, set the temperature to 225° F (107° C) and place the chicken breast in the wood pellet smoker. Smoke the chicken for an hour then transfer to a disposable aluminum pan.

4. Quickly combine honey with maple syrup then stir until incorporated. Drizzle half of the honey mixture over the chicken breast then sprinkle brown sugar on top.

5. Flip the chicken breast then coat the other side of the chicken with honey mixture and brown sugar. Place the disposable aluminum pan with chicken inside in the wood pellet smoker then smoke for about 2 hours. After 2 hours, check if the internal

temperature has reached 165° F (74° C). Add more time if it is necessary.

6. Once the chicken is done, take the disposable aluminum pan from the wood pellet smoker and let it rest for a few minutes. Using a fork or a sharp knife shred the smoked chicken then place it on a serving dish. Drizzle the liquid over the smoked chicken then stir a bit. Serve and enjoy.

Nutrition:

- Calories: 201.

- Carbohydrates: 0 g.

- Fat: 18 g.

- Protein: 34 g.

60. Natural White Smoked Chicken Breast

Preparation time: 10 minutes.

Cooking time: 2 hours 15 minutes.

Servings: 4

Ingredients:

- ✓ Boneless chicken breast (4.5-lbs., 2 kg.)
- ✓ 3 tbsp. injection vegetable oil.
- ✓ ¼ cup chicken broth.
- ✓ 2 tbsp. Worcestershire sauce.
- ✓ ¾ tbsp. salt.
- ✓ 1 ½ tsp. garlic powder.
- ✓ 1 ½ tsp. onion powder.
- ✓ ¾ tsp. bay leaf.
- ✓ ¾ tsp. thyme.
- ✓ ¾ tsp. sage.
- ✓ ¾ tsp. black pepper.
- ✓ 2 tbsp. rub salt.
- ✓ 3 tbsp. minced garlic.
- ✓ 1 tbsp. minced ginger.
- ✓ 3 tbsp. lemon juice.

For the heat:

✓ Pecan wood pellets

Preparation:

1. Pour vegetable oil and chicken broth into a bowl then season with Worcestershire sauce, salt, garlic powder, onion powder, bay leaf, thyme, sage, and black pepper. Stir the liquid until incorporated.

2. Fill an injector with the liquid mixture then inject the chicken breast at several places.

3. After that, combine the salt, minced garlic, minced ginger, and lemon juice in a bowl. Stir the spices until well mixed. Rub the chicken breast with the spice mixture then let it rest for an hour. Next, plug the wood pellet smoker and place the wood pellet inside the hopper.

4. Turn the switch on. Set the smoke setting and prepare the wood pellet smoker for indirect heat. Once the wood pellet smoker is ready, set the temperature to 250° F (121° C) and place the chicken breast in the wood pellet smoker. Smoke the chicken for 2 hours and once the internal temperature has reached 165° F (74° C), remove the smoked chicken from the wood pellet smoker.

5. Quickly wrap the smoked chicken with aluminum foil then let it rest for approximately an hour or so. After an hour, unwrap the smoked chicken then cut

it into thick slices. Arrange the sliced smoked chicken on a serving dish then serve immediately.

6. Enjoy!

Nutrition:

- Calories: 232.

- Carbohydrates: 0 g.

- Fat: 24 g.

- Protein: 23 g.

61. Wood Pellet Chicken

Preparation time: 6 minutes.

Cooking time: 30 minutes.

Servings: 5–6

Ingredients:

- ✓ 1 chopped frying chicken.
- ✓ 1 large egg.
- ✓ 1 tbsp. baking powder.
- ✓ 1 tbsp. paprika.
- ✓ ½ tsp. pepper.
- ✓ ½ tsp. salt.
- ✓ ½ tsp. of seasoned salt.
- ✓ ½ cup of evaporated milk.
- ✓ ¾ cup of all-purpose flour.

Preparation:

1. Beat the eggs in a small bowl; then add the evaporated milk and thoroughly stir.

2. Combine the flour with the paprika, the baking powder, the salts, and the pepper in a large bowl.

3. In a small bowl, melt the butter in a microwave; then pour it into a large shallow baking tray

4. Dip the chicken pieces in the mixture of milk and eggs; then roll it into the mixture of the flour

5. Place the chicken pieces in your wood pellet smoker grill over the grilling grate

6. When the temperature stabilizes, cook the chicken pieces for about 25 minutes

7. Let the chicken rest for about 5 minutes

8. Serve and enjoy your dish!

Nutrition:

- Calories: 377.

- Fat: 21 g.

- Carbohydrates: 4.4 g.

- Protein: 20 g.

- Fiber: 0.1 g.

62. Fruit Stuffed Chicken

Preparation time: 20 minutes.

Cooking time: 90 minutes.

Servings: 5

Ingredients:

- ✓ 1 chicken of about 4–5 lbs.
- ✓ 1 fresh chopped pineapple.
- ✓ GMG roasted garlic chipotle dry rub.
- ✓ 3–4 tbsp. pineapple jam.

Preparation:

1. Sprinkle the dry rub GMG roasted garlic chipotle on top of the chicken and into the cavity.
2. Stuff the cavity of the chicken with the wedges of the pineapple.
3. Smoke the chicken at a temperature of about 150° F for about 1 hour.
4. Increase the temperature to about 350° F and smoke grill for about 30 minutes.
5. Let the chicken rest for about 5 minutes.

6. Serve and enjoy your dish!

Nutrition:

- Calories: 252.3.
- Fat: 12.02 g.
- Carbohydrates: 21 g.
- Protein: 14.6 g.
- Dietary fiber: 1.3 g.

63. BBQ Chicken

Preparation time: 10 minutes.

Cooking time: 3 hours.

Servings: 4

Ingredients:

- ✓ 2 lbs. of the whole chicken.
- ✓ 6 chilies, Thai chili.
- ✓ 1 tsp. of paprika, sweet.
- ✓ 1 scotch bonnet.
- ✓ 2 tbsp. of brown sugar.
- ✓ Salt, to taste.
- ✓ 1 onion, chopped.
- ✓ 5 garlic cloves, minced.
- ✓ 4 cups of olive oil.

Preparation:

1. Put the Thai chili, paprika, bonnet, brown sugar, onion, garlic, and salt along with olive oil in the food processor.

2. Now marinate the chicken by smothering it with the puree.

3. Let it sit for a few hours in the refrigerator for marinating.

4. When ready to cook, set the temperate for 300° F and close the lid and preheat the grill for 20 minutes.

5. Next, place the chicken on the grill, breast side up, and smoke for 3 hours.

6. Once, the internal temperate reaches 165° F.

7. Once the time completes, flip to cook from the other side.

8. Remove it from the grill and allow it to cool for 10 minutes.

9. Serve and enjoy.

Nutrition:

- Calories: 167.
- Total fat: 24 g.
- Saturated fat: 8.5 g.
- Protein: 34 g.
- Carbohydrates: 1 g.

64. Balsamic Vinegar Chicken Breasts

Preparation time: 10 minutes.

Cooking time: 3 hours.

Servings: 4

Ingredients:

- ✓ 6 tbsp. olive oil.
- ✓ 1 cup balsamic vinegar.
- ✓ 3 cloves garlic cloves, minced.
- ✓ 1 tsp. basil leaves, fresh.
- ✓ 1 tsp. chili powder.
- ✓ Salt and black pepper, to taste.
- ✓ 2 lbs. chicken breast, boneless and skinless.

Preparation:

1. In a zip lock bag, add oil, balsamic vinegar, basil leaves, chili powder, garlic cloves, salt, and black pepper.

2. Now, place the chicken in the zip lock bag and mix well.

3. Marinate the chicken in the sauce, for 3 hours in the refrigerator.

4. Now, preheat the grill for 20 minutes at 225° F.

5. Place the chicken onto the grill, and smoke for 3 hours.

6. Once the internal temperature reached 150°, remove it from the grill, and then let it get cool for 10 minutes before serving.

7. Serve and enjoy.

Nutrition:

- Calories: 105.
- Total fat: 33 g.
- Saturated fat: 7.5 g.
- Protein: 22 g.
- Carbohydrates: 0 g.

65. Herbed Smoked Hen

Preparation time: 10 minutes.

Cooking time: 50 minutes.

Servings: 5

Ingredients:

- ✓ 12 cups of filtered water.

- ✓ 3 cups of beer nonalcoholic.

- ✓ Sea salt, to taste.

- ✓ ⅓ cup brown sugar.

- ✓ 2 tbsp. of rosemary.

- ✓ ½ tsp. of sage.

- ✓ 25 lbs. of a whole chicken, trimmed and giblets removed.

- ✓ 6 tbsp. butter.

- ✓ 2 tbsp. olive oil, for basting.

- ✓ 1/3 cup Italian seasoning.

- ✓ 1 tbsp. garlic powder.

- ✓ 1 tbsp. lemon zest.

Preparation:

1. Pour water into a large cooking pot and then add sugar and salt to the water.

2. Boil the water until the sugar and salt dissolve.

3. Now to the boiling water, add rosemary and sage.

4. Boil it until the aroma comes.

5. Now pour the beer into the water and then submerge the chicken into the boiling water.

6. Turn off the heat and refrigerate the chicken for a few hours.

7. After few hours removed it from the brine, and then pat dry with the paper towel.

8. Let the chicken sit for a few minutes at room temperature.

9. Now rub the chicken with the butter and massage it completely for fine coating.

10. Season the chicken with garlic powder, lemon zest, and Italian seasoning.

11. Preheat the Electrical smoker at 270° F until the smoke started to build.

12. Baste the chicken with olive oil and put it on the grill grate.

13. Cook the chicken with the lid closed, for 30–40 minutes, or until the internal temperature reaches 165° F.

14. Serve and enjoy.

Nutrition:

- Calories: 153.
- Total fat: 16 g.
- Saturated fat: 16.5 g.
- Protein: 15 g.
- Carbohydrates: 2 g.
- Fiber: 0 g.
- Sugar: 5 g.

66. Smoked Chicken Thighs

Preparation time: 10 minutes.

Cooking time: 2 hours.

Servings: 4

Ingredients:

- ✓ 2.5 lbs. of chicken thighs.
- ✓ 4 tbsp. soy sauce.
- ✓ 4 tsp. sesame oil.
- ✓ 2 garlic cloves.
- ✓ 1-inch ginger, grated.
- ✓ 1 small white onion, chopped.
- ✓ ½ tbsp. thyme.
- ✓ 2 tsp. allspice, powder.
- ✓ ½ tsp. cinnamon.
- ✓ ½ tsp. crushed red chili peppers, powder.

Preparation:

1. Take a food processor and add soy sauce, sesame oil, garlic cloves, ginger, onions, thyme, allspice powder, cinnamon, and red chili peppers.

2. Blend the mixture into a smooth paste.

3. Coat the chicken thighs with the blended paste, and marinate in a zip-lock plastic bag for 2 hours in the refrigerator.

4. Preheat the smoker at 225° F, until the smoke started to form.

5. Place the chicken directly onto the grill grate, and cook the chicken for 2 hours.

6. Use a thermometer to read the internal temperature of the chicken.

7. Once the temperature reaches 145° F, the chicken is ready to be served

8. Remove the chicken from the gill great, and let it sit at room temperature for 20 minutes, before serving.

9. Serve and enjoy.

Nutrition:

- Calories: 267.
- Total fat: 19 g.
- Saturated fat: 4.5 g.
- Protein: 29 g.
- Carbohydrates: 10 g.
- Fiber: 0 g.
- Sugar: 0 g.

67. Maple Glazed Whole Chicken

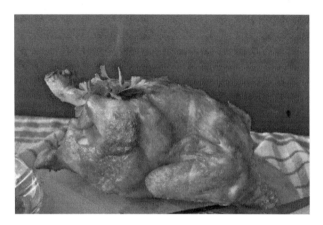

Preparation time: 10 minutes.

Cooking time: 3 hours.

Servings: 4

Ingredients:

- ✓ 2.5 lbs. whole chicken.
- ✓ 4 tbsp. of melted butter.
- ✓ 1 cup of grapefruit juice.
- ✓ 2.5 cups chicken stock.

Ingredients for the rub:

- ✓ Black pepper and salt, to taste.
- ✓ 3 garlic cloves, minced.

✓ 3 tsp. onion powder.   ✓ ½ tsp. 5-spice powder.

✓ 1.5 tsp. ginger,
  minced.

Ingredients for the glaze:

✓ 6 tsp. coconut milk.   ✓ 1 tbsp. lemon juice.

✓ 3 tbsp. sesame oil.   ✓ 4 tbsp. melted butter.

✓ 3 tbsp. maple syrup.

Preparation:

1. In a small cooking pot, pour the coconut milk and add sesame oil, maple syrup, melted butter, and lemon juice.

2. Cook the mixture for a few minutes until all the ingredients are combined well, the glaze is ready.

3. Reserve some of the mixture for further use.

4. Take a separate cooking pot and add chicken stock, butter, and grapefruit juice.

5. Simmer the mixture for a few minutes, and then add the chicken to this liquid.

6. Submerge the chicken completely in the brain and let it sit for a few hours for marinating.

7. In a separate bowl, combine all the rub ingredients.

8. After a few hours pass, take out the chicken from the liquid and pat dry with a paper towel.

9. Now cover the chicken with the rub mixture.

10. Preheat the smoker grill for 20 minutes at 225° F.

11. Cherry or apple wood chips can be used to create the smoke.

12. Place chicken onto the smoker grill grate and cook for 3 hours by closing the lid.

13. After every 30 minutes, baste the chicken with the maple glaze.

14. Once the internal temperature of the chicken reaches 165° F the chicken is ready to be served.

15. Remove the chicken from the grill grate and baste it with the glaze and additional butter on top.

16. Let the chicken sit at room temperature for 10 minutes before cutting and serving.

Nutrition:

- Calories: 227.
- Total fat: 14 g.
- Saturated fat: 4.5 g.
- Protein: 17 g.
- Carbohydrates: 8 g.
- Fiber: 0 g.
- Sugar: 2 g.

68. Sriracha Chicken Wings

Preparation time: 10 minutes.

Cooking time: 2 hours.

Servings: 4

Ingredients:

- ✓ 2 lbs. of chicken wings.
- ✓ 2 tsp. garlic powder.
- ✓ Sea salt, to taste.
- ✓ Freshly ground black pepper, to taste.

Ingredients for the sauce:

- 1/3 cup raw honey.

- 1/3 cup Sriracha sauce.

- 2 tbsp. coconut amino.

- 3 limes, juice only.

Preparation:

1. Take a large mixing bowl and combine the sauce ingredients including Sriracha sauce, raw honey, coconut amino, and lime juice.

2. Rub the chicken with salt, black pepper, and garlic powder.

3. Preheat the smoker grill for 30 minutes at 225° F.

4. Put the chicken directly onto the grill grate and smoke with the closed lid for 2 hours.

5. When the internal temperature reaches 150° F the chicken is ready.

6. Remove the chicken from the grill grate and dumped into the sauce bowl.

7. Toss the chicken wings well for the fine coating.

8. Serve and enjoy.

Nutrition:

- Calories: 107.

- Total fat: 10 g.

- Saturated fat: 0.9 g.

- Protein: 15 g.

- Carbohydrates: 2 g.

- Fiber: 0 g.

- Sugar: 0 g.

69. Rosemary Chicken

Preparation time: 4 hours 10 minutes.

Cooking time: 1 hour 5 minutes.

Servings: 6

Ingredients:

- ✓ 4 lbs. chicken thighs, boneless.
- ✓ 2 tsp. garlic powder.
- ✓ 2 tsp. salt.
- ✓ 1/2 cup brown sugar.
- ✓ 1 tsp. ground black pepper.
- ✓ 4 tsp. fresh rosemary, chopped.
- ✓ 1/4 cup soy sauce.
- ✓ 1/2 cup apple cider vinegar.
- ✓ 1/2 cup Worcestershire sauce.
- ✓ 1/2 cup olive oil.
- ✓ 1/2 of a lemon, juiced.
- ✓ 1/4 cup Dijon mustard.

Preparation:

1. Place all the ingredients in a small bowl, except for chicken, and then stir well until combined.

2. Place chicken thighs in a large plastic bag, pour in the prepared mixture, seal the bag, turn it upside down to coat the chicken pieces, and let marinate in the refrigerator for a minimum of 4 hours.

3. When ready to cook, open the hopper of the smoker, add dry pallets, make sure the ash-can is in place, then open the ash damper, power on the smoker, and close the ash damper.

4. Set the temperature of the smoker to 350° F, let preheat for 30 minutes or until the green light on the dial blinks that indicate the smoker has reached to set temperature.

5. Remove chicken thighs from the marinade, place them on the smoker grill, shut with lid, and smoke for 35 minutes or until thoroughly cooked and the internal temperature of chicken reaches 165° F.

6. When done, transfer chicken to a dish and serve straight away.

Nutrition:

- Calories: 109.

- Total fat: 5.5 g.

- Saturated fat: 1.1 g.

- Protein: 13.7 g.

- Carbohydrates: 0.6 g.

- Fiber: 0.2 g.

- Sugar: 0.1 g.

FISH AND
SEAFOOD
RECIPES

70. Grilled Fish

Low on fat and calories but full of flavor—this grilled fish recipe is a welcome addition to your weekly menu.

Preparation time: 1 hour 20 minutes.

Servings: 4

Ingredients:

- ✓ ¼ cup olive oil.
- ✓ 1 cup soy sauce.
- ✓ 3 sprigs basil, chopped.
- ✓ 2 tbsp. lemon juice.
- ✓ 1 tbsp. garlic, minced.
- ✓ 4 lb. fish, sliced.

Preparation:

1. In a bowl, mix the olive oil, soy sauce, basil, lemon juice, and garlic.

2. Stir in the fish and coat with the sauce.

3. Cover and marinate for 45 minutes.

4. Preheat your wood pellet grill to 350° F.

5. Close the lid for 10 minutes.

6. Add the fish to the grill.

7. Cook for 20 minutes.

Nutrition:

- Calories: 612.

- Fat: 17.8 g.

- Saturated fat: 4.1 g.

- Carbohydrates: 5.7 g.

- Dietary fiber: 0.6 g.

- Protein: 109.3 g.

- Cholesterol: 275 mg.

- Sugars: 1.3 g.

- Sodium: 3796 mg.

- Potassium: 160 mg.

71. Grilled Swordfish Fillet With Basil Orange Pesto

Whitefish fillet infused with orange and basil pesto for a dinner that's memorable for everyone.

Preparation time: 30 minutes.

Servings: 6

Ingredients:

- ✓ ½ cup olive oil.
- ✓ 1 cup parsley, chopped.
- ✓ 2 cups basil, fresh.
- ✓ 2 tsp. orange zest.
- ✓ 2 tbsp. orange juice.
- ✓ ½ cup walnuts, toasted.
- ✓ 1 cup parmesan cheese, grated.
- ✓ Salt and pepper to taste.
- ✓ 4 swordfish steaks.
- ✓ 1 tbsp. olive oil.

Preparation:

1. Preheat your wood pellet grill to high.
2. Close the lid for 15 minutes.

3. Add the olive oil, parsley, basil, orange zest, orange juice, and walnuts to a food processor.

4. Pulse until smooth.

5. Transfer to a bowl.

6. Stir in the parmesan cheese, salt, and pepper.

7. Brush both sides of the swordfish with olive oil.

8. Sprinkle with salt and pepper.

9. Grill for 15 minutes.

10. Spread the pesto on top of the fish and serve.

Nutrition:

- Calories: 368.

- Fat: 29.2 g.

- Saturated fat: 5.4 g.

- Cholesterol: 44 mg.

- Sugars: 0.7 g

- Carbohydrates: 2.6 g

- Dietary fiber: 1.3 g

- Protein: 24.4 g.

- Sodium: 254 mg.

- Potassium: 406 mg.

72. Roasted Fish With Veggies

This is 1 seafood dish that's so easy to get addicted to—roasted yellowtail fish with mushrooms and potatoes and served with Italian salsa verde.

Preparation time: 1 hour.

Servings: 4

Ingredients:

- ✓ 4 yellowtail fillets.
- ✓ 4 tbsp. olive oil, divided.
- ✓ Salt and pepper to taste.
- ✓ 1 lb. mushrooms.
- ✓ 1 lb. baby potatoes.
- ✓ 2 tbsp. fresh mint leaves.
- ✓ 1 tbsp. cilantro, chopped.
- ✓ ½ cup parsley, chopped.
- ✓ 2 cloves garlic, minced.
- ✓ 1 tbsp. oregano, chopped.
- ✓ Pinch crushed red pepper.
- ✓ Lemon juice.

Preparation:

1. Preheat your wood pellet grill to high.

2. Close the lid for 10 minutes.

3. Add a cast-iron skillet to the grill.

4. Heat it for 15 minutes.

5. While waiting, drizzle the fish with half of the olive oil.

6. Sprinkle both sides with salt and pepper.

7. Toss the mushrooms and potatoes in the remaining olive oil.

8. Season with salt and pepper.

9. Add the potatoes and mushrooms to the pan.

10. Cook for 10 minutes, stirring often.

11. Add the fish to the grill grate.

12. Cook the fish for 5 minutes per side.

13. In a bowl, combine the mint leaves, cilantro, parsley, garlic, oregano, red pepper flakes, and lemon juice.

14. Serve the fish, mushrooms, and potatoes with the salsa verde on the side.

Nutrition:

- Calories: 431.

- Fat: 25.8 g.

- Saturated fat: 4.7 g.

- Carbohydrates: 35.3 g.

- Dietary fiber: 5.4 g.

- Protein: 20.4 g.

- Cholesterol: 31 mg.

- Sugars: 2.1 g.

- Sodium: 508 mg.

- Potassium: 1203 mg.

73. Grilled Salmon

Preparation time: 10 minutes.

Cooking time: 30 minutes.

Servings: 6

Ingredients:

- ✓ 2 lbs. salmon (cut into fillets).
- ✓ 1/2 cup low sodium soy sauce.
- ✓ 2 garlic cloves (grated).
- ✓ 4 tbsp. olive oil.
- ✓ 2 tbsp. honey.
- ✓ 1 tsp. ground black pepper.
- ✓ ½ tsp. smoked paprika.
- ✓ ½ tsp. Italian seasoning.

For the garnish:

- ✓ 2 tbsp. chopped green onion.

Preparation:

1. In a huge container, combine the honey, pepper, paprika, Italian seasoning, garlic, soy sauce, and olive oil. Add the salmon fillets and toss to combine. Cover the bowl and refrigerate for 1 hour.

2. Remove the fillets from the marinade and let it sit for about 2 hours, or until it is at room temperature.

3. Start the wood pellet on smoke, leaving the lid opened for 5 minutes, or until fire starts.

4. Close the lid and preheat the grill to 350° F for 15 minutes.

5. Grease the grill grate with oil and arrange the fillets on the grill grate, skin side up. Close the grill lid and cook for 4 minutes.

6. Flip the fillets and cook for additional 25 minutes or until the fish is flaky.

7. Remove the fillets from heat and let them sit for a few minutes.

8. Serve warm and garnish with chopped green onion.

Nutrition:

- Calories 317.
- Fat 18.8 g.
- Carbohydrates: 8.3 g.
- Protein 30.6 g.

74. Smoked Salmon

Preparation time: 12 hours.

Cooking time: 4 hours.

Servings: 6

Ingredients:

For the brine:

- ✓ 4 cups water.
- ✓ 1 cup brown sugar.
- ✓ 1/3 cup kosher salt.

For the salmon:

- ✓ 1 large skin-on salmon filet.
- ✓ Real maple syrup.

Preparation:

1. Combine the ingredients of the brine until the sugar is completely dissolved; then place it into a large zip lock bag or a large covered container; then place the cleaned salmon into that brine, and refrigerate for about 10–12 hours.

2. Once the fish is perfectly brined, remove it from the liquid; then rinse and pat dry with clean paper towels.

3. Let the fish sit out at room temperature for about 1–2 hours to let the pellicle form.

4. Turn the smoker on to get the fire started; then place the salmon over a baking rack sprayed with cooking spray

5. Place the rack over the smoker; then close the lid

6. Baste the salmon with the pure syrup generously.

7. Smoke for about 3–4 hours; then serve and enjoy.

Nutrition:

- Calories: 101.

- Fat: 2 g.

- Carbs: 16 g.

- Protein: 4 g.

75. Smoked Sardines

Preparation time: 12 hours.

Cooking time: 5 hours.

Servings: 5

Ingredients:

- ✓ 20–30 fresh gutted sardines.
- ✓ 4 cups water.
- ✓ ¼ cup kosher salt.
- ✓ ¼ cup honey.
- ✓ 4–5 bay leaves.
- ✓ 1 chopped or finely grated onion.
- ✓ 2 smashed garlic cloves.
- ✓ ½ cup chopped parsley or cilantro.
- ✓ 3–4 crushed dried or hot chilies.
- ✓ 2 tbsp. cracked black peppercorns.

Preparation:

1. Start by gutting and washing the sardines; then remove the backbone and the ribs.

2. In making a brine, put all the ingredients above except for the sardines in a pot; then bring the mixture to a boil and turn off the heat after that.

3. Stir your ingredients to combine; then cover and let come to room temperature.

4. When the brine is perfectly cool, submerge the sardines in it in a large, covered, and non-reactive container.

5. Let the sardines soak in the refrigerator for about 12 hours or overnight.

6. Take the sardines out of the brine; then rinse under the cold water quickly and pat dry.

7. Let dry over a rack in a cool place for about 30–60 minutes.

8. Be sure to turn the fish over once; then once the sardines look dry to you; place them in a smoker as far away from the heat as possible.

9. Smoke the sardines for about 4–5 hours over almond wood.

Nutrition:

- Calories: 180.
- Fat: 10 g.
- Carbs: 0 g.
- Protein: 13 g.

76. Smoked Catfish

Preparation time: 2 hours.

Cooking time: 2 hours 30 minutes.

Servings: 3

Ingredients:

- ✓ 4–5 catfish fillets.
- ✓ 1 cup of oil.
- ✓ ½ cup red wine vinegar.
- ✓ 1 juiced lemon.
- ✓ 1 minced garlic clove.
- ✓ 2 tbsp. oregano.
- ✓ 1 tbsp. thyme.
- ✓ 1 tbsp. basil.
- ✓ 1 tbsp. black pepper.
- ✓ 1 tbsp. cayenne pepper.
- ✓ 1 tbsp. salt.
- ✓ 3 tbsp. sugar.
- ✓ Wood of your choice.

Preparation:

1. Mix the ingredients of the marinade ingredients all together.

2. Place the catfish in a shallow baking bowl or dish

3. Pour the marinade on top of the fish and turn them to ensure that the catfish are evenly coated.

4. Cover your dish with plastic wrap and place it in the fridge for about 1 hour.

5. Start the smoker with the wood of your choice and set it aside for a temperature of about 225° F

6. Place the catfish over racks and place it in the smoker.

7. Smoke the catfish for about 2 and 1/3 hours.

Nutrition:

- Calories: 139.

- Fat: 5.37 g.

- Carbohydrates: 0 g.

- Protein: 21.5 g.

77. Smoked Ahi Tuna

Preparation time: 40 minutes.

Cooking time: 4 hours.

Servings: 6

Ingredients:

- ✓ 6 albacore tuna filets of about 8 oz.
- ✓ 1 cup kosher salt
- ✓ 1 cup brown sugar
- ✓ The zest of 1 orange.
- ✓ The zest of 1 lemon.

Preparation:

1. In a small bowl; combine altogether the salt with the sugar and the citrus zest.

2. Layer the fish and the brine in a container making sure that there is enough brine between each of the filet; then let the brine sit in the refrigerator for about 6 hours

3. Start your wood pellet smoker grill on smoke with the lid open for about 4–5 minutes

4. Leave the temperature setting on smoke and preheat for about 10–15 minutes

209

5. Remove the fillets from the brine and rinse any excess; then pat dry and place over a rack in the refrigerator for about 30–40 minutes

6. Remove the filets from the fridge and place them on the grill grate cooking for about 3 hours

7. Increase the temperature to about 225° F and cook for about 1 additional hour

8. Remove from the grill; then serve and enjoy your dish.

Nutrition:

- Calories: 150.
- Fat: 14.1 g.
- Carbs: 0.9 g.
- Protein: 4.8 g.

78. Smoked Flatbread Salmon

Preparation time: 20 minutes.

Cooking time: 45 minutes.

Servings: 4–6

Ingredients:

- ✓ 1 pizza dough.
- ✓ 1/4 cup crème Fraiche.
- ✓ 1/4 cup ricotta cheese.
- ✓ Salt.
- ✓ 1/2 chives, chopped.
- ✓ 1/2 kg smoked salmon.
- ✓ Capers, drained.
- ✓ Extra-virgin olive oil.

Preparation:

1. Heat the oven to 200° F.

2. Spread a little olive oil to the roasting pan.

3. Knead dough into a flat disk on a floured surface. Transfer dough to the prepared pan. Rub the top with olive oil and sprinkle with salt. Prick dough with a fork.

4. Bake the dough in a preheated oven for 5 minutes, then turn down the oven to 200° F. Bake for another 5–7 minutes until the crust is brown.

5. In the meantime, combine ricotta cheese, crème Fraiche, and chopped chives. Season with salt. Remove crust from oven and spread the mixture on top. Cover salmon with a thin layer of olive oil and place it on the bread. Bake at 200° F for 2 minutes.

6. Remove the bread from the oven, garnish with capers and drizzle with extra-virgin olive oil. Serve with a green salad.

Nutrition:

- Calories: 231.

- Protein: 19.56 g.

- Fat: 8.69 g.

- Carbohydrates: 11.81 g.

- Calcium: 204 mg.

- Magnesium: 29 mg.

- Phosphorus: 302 mg.

- Iron: 0.79 mg.

- Fiber: 0.2 g.

79. Smoked Seafood Ceviche

Preparation time: 20 minutes.

Cooking time: 45 minutes.

Servings: 4–6

Ingredients:

- ✓ 1-lb. sea scallops.
- ✓ 1-lb. shrimp.
- ✓ 1 tbsp. canola oil.
- ✓ 1 lime, zested and juiced.
- ✓ 1 lemon juice.
- ✓ 1 orange, juiced.
- ✓ 1 tsp. garlic powder.
- ✓ 1 tsp. onion powder.
- ✓ 2 tsp. black pepper.
- ✓ 1 tsp. salt.
- ✓ 1 avocado, diced.
- ✓ 12 red onion.
- ✓ 1 tbsp. cilantro.
- ✓ 1 pinch red pepper flakes.

Preparation:

1. Smoke shrimp until crustaceans are just done, set aside to cool. Shuck scallops, dice and marinate with red onion and allow seafood to chill in the refrigerator for 1 hour.

2. Chill avocado and stir into the rest of the ingredients. Serve it chilled.

Nutrition:

- Calories: 334.

- Protein: 34.5 g.

- Fat: 9.21 g.

- Carbohydrates: 30.69 g.

- Calcium: 181 mg.

- Magnesium: 90 mg.

- Phosphorus: 561 mg.

- Iron: 2.94 mg.

80. Baked Halibut Fish Sticks With Spicy Coleslaw

Preparation time: 20 minutes.

Cooking time: 35 minutes

Servings: 4–6

Ingredients:

- ✓ 1/2 cup mayonnaise.
- ✓ 1/2 cup sour cream.
- ✓ 1/2 tbsp. salt.
- ✓ Black pepper.
- ✓ 2 tbsp. dill seed.
- ✓ 1 tbsp. sugar.
- ✓ 2 tbsp. sriracha.
- ✓ 2 tbsp. white wine vinegar.
- ✓ 1 head cabbage, shredded.
- ✓ 1 large carrot, peeled, shaved thin.
- ✓ Olive oil.
- ✓ 1 1/2-lb. halibut.
- ✓ 1/2 cup all-purpose flour.
- ✓ 1/2 breadcrumbs.

Preparation:

1. Make the spicy coleslaw by combining the sour cream, mayonnaise, salt, pepper, dill, sugar, sriracha, and vinegar together in a large bowl. Then mix in the cabbage and carrots. Cover the bowl and keep it refrigerated until you are ready to serve.

2. Add the olive oil into a large skillet over medium-high heat until it is nice and hot.

3. Season the halibut fillets with salt and pepper on both sides.

4. Dip the fish into the batter and then dredge it into the flour. Remove any excess flour.

5. Lift the batter-coated fish out of the bowl and allow any excess batter to drip off.

6. Add the fish and cook it until it's opaque and firm to touch, about 2–4 minutes per side.

7. Serve it with a bed of spicy coleslaw and/or a lemon wedge.

Nutrition:

- Calories: 386.

- Protein: 21.05 g.

- Fat: 24.69 g.

- Carbohydrates: 20.63 g.

- Calcium: 123 mg.

- Magnesium: 67 mg.

- Phosphorus: 260 mg.

- Iron: 2.47 mg.

81. Spicy Shrimps Skewers

Preparation time: 10 minutes.

Cooking time: 6 minutes.

Servings: 4

Ingredients:

✓ 2 lbs. shrimp, peeled, and deveined

For the marinade:

✓ 6 oz. Thai chilies.

✓ 6 cloves of garlic, peeled.

✓ 1 ½ tsp. sugar.

✓ 2 tbsp. napa valley rub.

✓ 1 ½ tbsp. white vinegar.

✓ 3 tbsp. olive oil.

Preparation:

1. Prepare the marinade and for this, place all of its ingredients in a food processor and then pulse for 1 minute until smooth.

2. Take a large bowl, place shrimps on it, add prepared marinade, toss until well coated, and let marinate for a minimum of 30 minutes in the refrigerator.

3. When ready to cook, switch on the Traeger grill, fill the grill hopper with apple-flavored wood pellets, power the grill on by using the control panel, select smoke on the temperature dial, or set the temperature to 450° F and let it preheat for a minimum of 5 minutes.

4. Meanwhile, remove shrimps from the marinade and then thread onto skewers.

5. When the grill has preheated, open the lid, place shrimps' skewers on the grill grate, shut the grill, and smoke for 3 minutes per side until firm.

6. When done, transfer shrimps' skewers to a dish and then serve.

Nutrition:

- Calories: 187.2.
- Fat: 2.7 g.
- Carbs: 2.7 g.
- Protein: 23.2 g.
- Fiber: 0.2 g.

82. Tuna Tacos

Preparation time: 10 minutes.

Cooking time: 35 minutes.

Servings: 4

Ingredients:

- ✓ 1.5 kg of tuna.
- ✓ 3 tbsp. olive oil.
- ✓ 1/4 cup of spices for fish.
- ✓ 1 piece of grated ginger root.
- ✓ 3 tbsp. vinegar.
- ✓ 1 tbsp. honey.
- ✓ 1 tbsp. red pepper flakes.
- ✓ 1/2 tsp. salt.
- ✓ 1/4 tsp. ground black pepper.
- ✓ 1 fresh anna (already cleaned and finely chopped).
- ✓ 1 cabbage (grated).

✓ 2 carrots (grated).

✓ 12 tortillas (you can also use the piadina).

✓ 3 spoons of cilantro (chopped).

Preparation:

1. Preheat the barbecue to 230° C and prepare it for the grill, close the lid, and leave it for about 15 minutes.

2. Brush the tuna with a light layer of olive oil and then cover it with a layer of spice for fish, let the tuna marinate for 10 minutes while preparing the cabbage salad.

3. For the salad, mix ginger, vinegar, honey, pepper flakes, salt, and pepper, then in a large bowl combined with the pineapple, carrots, and cabbage.

4. Grate the tuna for 3 minutes on each side, then remove it from the grill and let it rest for 5 minutes before continuing to fray it.

5. At this point you can fill the tortillas (or piadina) with tuna and coleslaw, the tacos are ready to serve them.

Nutrition:

- Calories: 290.
- Fat: 22 g.
- Carbohydrates: 1 g.
- Protein: 20 g.
- Fiber: 0.3 g.

83. Lemon Garlic Scallops

Preparation time: 10 minutes.

Cooking time: 5 minutes.

Servings: 6

Ingredients:

- ✓ 1 dozen scallops.
- ✓ 2 tbsp. chopped parsley.
- ✓ Salt as needed.
- ✓ 1 tbsp. olive oil.
- ✓ 1 tbsp. butter, unsalted.
- ✓ 1 tsp. lemon zest.

For the garlic butter:

- ✓ ½ tsp. minced garlic.

- ✓ 1 lemon, juiced.

- ✓ 4 tbsp. butter, unsalted, melted.

Preparation:

1. Switch on the Traeger grill, fill the grill hopper with alder flavored wood pellets, power the grill on by using the control panel, select smoke on the temperature dial, or set the temperature to 400° F and let it preheat for a minimum of 15 minutes.

2. Meanwhile, remove the grill from scallops, pat dry with paper towels, and then season with salt and black pepper. When the grill has preheated, open the lid, place a skillet on the grill grate, add butter and oil, and when the butter melts, place seasoned scallops on it and then cook for 2 minutes until seared. Meanwhile, prepare the garlic butter and for this, take a small bowl, place all of its ingredients in it and then whisk until combined.

3. Flip the scallops, top with some of the prepared garlic butter, and cook for another minute. When done, transfer scallops to a dish, top with remaining garlic butter, sprinkle with parsley and lemon zest, and then serve.

Nutrition:

- Calories: 184.
- Fat: 10 g.
- Carbs: 1 g.
- Protein: 22 g.
- Fiber: 0.2 g.

82. Halibut in Parchment

Preparation time: 15 minutes.

Cooking time: 15 minutes.

Servings: 4

Ingredients:

- ✓ 16 asparagus spears, trimmed, sliced into 1/2-inch pieces.

- ✓ 2 ears of corn kernels.

- ✓ 4 oz. halibut fillets, pin bones removed.

- ✓ 2 lemons, cut into 12 slices.

- ✓ Salt as needed.

- ✓ Ground black pepper as needed.

- ✓ 2 tbsp. olive oil.

- ✓ 2 tbsp. chopped parsley.

Preparation:

1. Switch on the Traeger grill, fill the grill hopper with flavored wood pellets, power the grill on by using the control panel, select smoke on the temperature dial, or set the temperature to 450° F and let it preheat for a minimum of 5 minutes.

2. Meanwhile, cut out 18-inch-long parchment paper, place a fillet in the center of each parchment, season with salt and black pepper, and then drizzle with oil. Cover each fillet with 3 lemon slices, overlapping slightly, sprinkle 1-fourth of asparagus and corn on each fillet, season with some salt and black pepper, and seal the fillets and vegetables tightly to prevent steam from escaping the packet.

3. When the grill has preheated, open the lid, place fillet packets on the grill grate, shut the grill, and smoke for 15 minutes until packets have turned slightly brown and puffed up.

4. When done, transfer packets to a dish, let them stand for 5 minutes, then cut X in the center of each packet, carefully uncover the fillets and vegetables, sprinkle with parsley, and then serve.

Nutrition

- Calories: 186.6.
- Fat: 2.8 g.

- Carbohydrates: 14.2 g.

- Protein: 25.7 g.

- Fiber: 4.1 g.

83. Chilean Sea Bass

Preparation time: 30 minutes.

Cooking time: 40 minutes.

Servings: 6

Ingredients:

- ✓ 4 sea bass fillets, skinless, each about 6 oz.

- ✓ Chicken rub as needed.

- ✓ 8 tbsp. butter, unsalted.

- ✓ 2 tbsp. chopped thyme leaves.

- ✓ Lemon slices for serving.

For the marinade:

- ✓ 1 lemon, juiced.
- ✓ 4 tsp. minced garlic.
- ✓ 1 tbsp. chopped thyme.
- ✓ 1 tsp. blackened rub.
- ✓ 1 tbsp. chopped oregano.
- ✓ 1/4 cup oil.

Preparation:

1. Prepare the marinade and for this, take a small bowl, place all of its ingredients in it, stir until well combined, and then pour the mixture into a large plastic bag.

2. Add fillets in the bag, seal it, turn it upside down to coat fillets with the marinade and let it marinate for a minimum of 30 minutes in the refrigerator.

3. When ready to cook, switch on the Traeger grill, fill the grill hopper with apple-flavored wood pellets, power the grill on by using the control panel, select 'smoke' on the temperature dial, or set the temperature to 325° F and let it preheat for a minimum of 15 minutes.

4. Meanwhile, take a large baking pan and place butter on it. When the grill has preheated, open the lid, place the baking pan on the grill grate, and wait until butter melts.

5. When done, transfer fillets to a dish, sprinkle with thyme, then serve with lemon slices.

Nutrition

- Calories: 232.

- Fat: 12.2 g.

- Carbohydrates: 0.8 g.

- Protein: 28.2 g.

- Fiber: 0.1 g.

84. Sriracha Salmon

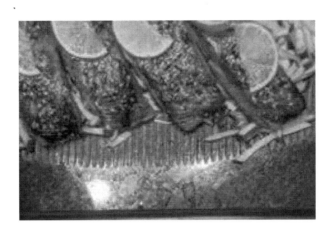

Preparation time: 2 hours 10 minutes.

Cooking time: 25 minutes.

Servings: 4

Ingredients:

- ✓ 3-lb. salmon, skin on.

For the marinade:

- ✓ 1 tsp. lime zest.
- ✓ 1 tbsp. minced garlic.
- ✓ 1 tbsp. grated ginger.
- ✓ Sea salt as needed.
- ✓ Ground black pepper as needed.
- ✓ 1/4 cup maple syrup.
- ✓ 2 tbsp. soy sauce.

- ✓ 2 tbsp. Sriracha sauce.
- ✓ 1 tbsp. rice vinegar.
- ✓ 1 tbsp. toasted sesame oil.
- ✓ 1 tsp. toasted sesame seeds.

Preparation:

1. Prepare the marinade and for this, take a small bowl, place all of its ingredients in it, stir until well combined, and then pour the mixture into a large plastic bag.

2. Add salmon in the bag, seal it, turn it upside down to coat salmon with the marinade and let it marinate for a minimum of 2 hours in the refrigerator.

3. When ready to cook, switch on the Traeger grill, fill the grill hopper with flavored wood pellets, power the grill on by using the control panel, select smoke on the temperature dial, or set the temperature to 450° F and let it preheat for a minimum of 5 minutes.

4. Meanwhile, take a large baking sheet, line it with parchment paper, place salmon on its skin-side down and then brush with the marinade.

5. When the grill has preheated, open the lid, place a baking sheet containing salmon on the grill grate, shut the grill, and smoke for 25 minutes until thoroughly cooked.

6. When done, transfer salmon to a dish and then serve.

Nutrition:

- Calories: 360.

- Fat: 21 g.

- Carbohydrates: 28 g.

- Protein: 16 g.

- Fiber: 1.5 g.

85. Smoked Fish Chowder

Preparation time: 20 minutes.

Cooking time: 35 minutes.

Servings: 4

Ingredients:

- ✓ 12-oz. skin-on salmon fillet.
- ✓ Traeger fin and feather rub.
- ✓ 2 corn husks.
- ✓ 3 slices bacon.
- ✓ 4 cans cream of potato soup, condensed.
- ✓ 3 cups whole milk.
- ✓ 8 oz. cream cheese.
- ✓ 3 green onions.
- ✓ 2 tsp. hot sauce.

Preparation:

1. Soak corn husks in warm water for 20 minutes. Remove from water promptly and pat dry.

2. Add a small handful of the Traeger fin and feather salmon rub to coat both sides of the salmon.

3. Combine smoked salmon, cream of potato soup, milk, cream cheese, corn starch, and green onions in a saucepan on medium heat, stirring and cooking until thickened and bubbly, about 10–15 minutes.

4. Stir in bacon and add hot sauce. Cook for 1 minute, then remove from heat.

5. Cut corn husks in half. Layer fish chowder in a circular design within 1 half of the husk.

6. Top with shredded cheddar cheese, fold in half and secure with a couple of toothpicks. Braais for 10–15 minutes or until the chowder is hot and cheese is melted.

7. Serve with a side of cornbread and enjoy it!

Nutrition:

- Calories: 839.

- Protein: 46.58 g.

- Fat: 45.25 g.

- Carbohydrates: 63.18 g.

- Calcium: 340 mg.

- Magnesium: 67 mg.

- Phosphorus: 597 mg.

- Iron: 4.79 mg.

86. Roasted Clambake

Preparation time: 20 minutes.

Cooking time: 1 hour 10 minutes.

Servings: 6–8.

Ingredients:

- ✓ 8 small potatoes.

- ✓ 1 potato, red.

- ✓ 2 yellow onions, quartered.

- ✓ 16 clams, in the shell.

- ✓ 16 mussels.

- ✓ 4 pieces of ears fresh corn 4 mild Italian sausage.

- ✓ 1 cup white wine.

- ✓ 3 cloves garlic.

- ✓ 2 whole lobsters.

- ✓ 1/2 cup butter, melted.

- ✓ 1 bread, French.

Preparation:

1. Clean the clams and mussels, but do not de-beard them, as it will make them taste like sand.

2. Place a heavy roasting pan in the oven, preheated to 300 degrees.

3. Prepare the sausage.

4. Add the wine and garlic.

5. Take the sausage and break it up into its individual pieces; add this to the roasting pan.

6. Bake in the oven for 1 hour.

7. When the hour is up, remove the roasting pan from the oven. Pour the butter over all the vegetables and meat. Return the roasting pan to the oven for another 10 minutes.

8. During this time, bring a pot of water to a boil. Place the ears of corn in the boiling water for 5 minutes, or until they are cooked.

9. When 10 minutes is up, take the corn out of the boiling water. Remove the outer husks from each ear. Remove the husks but do not scrape the corn off of the cobs.

10. Remove the roasting pan from the oven. Arrange each ear of corn in the center of a serving dish. Place the clam mixture and sausage around the corn. Sprinkle the lobster over the top. Serve with melted butter.

Nutrition:

- Calories: 763.

- Protein: 28.33 g.

- Fat: 21.44 g.

- Carbohydrates: 119.91 g.

- Calcium: 138 mg.

- Magnesium: 203 mg.

- Phosphorus: 587 mg.

- Iron: 6.89 mg.

- Fiber: 15.3 g.

- Sugars total: 9.2 g.

- Starch: 85.46 g.

87. Grilled Blackened Saskatchewan Salmon

Preparation time: 20 minutes.

Cooking time: 30 minutes.

Servings: 4–6

Ingredients:

- ✓ 1 salmon fillet
- ✓ Zesty Italian dressing.
- ✓ Traeger blackened Saskatchewan rub.
- ✓ Lemon wedges.

Preparation:

1. Rub the salmon thoroughly with the blackened Saskatchewan rub. Grill or barbecue to the desired doneness. In a glass, mix equal parts of basil pesto and Zesty Italian dressing.

2. Serve and enjoy it!

Nutrition:

- Calories: 351.

- Protein: 34.57 g.

- Fat: 20.24 g.

- Carbohydrates: 5.3 g.

- Calcium: 336 mg.

- Magnesium: 52 mg.

- Phosphorus: 542 mg.

- Iron: 1.06 mg.

- Fiber: 1.87 g.

88. Sweet Mandarin Salmon

Preparation time: 5 minutes.

Cooking time: 10 minutes.

Servings: 2

Ingredients:

- ✓ 1 whole lime juice.
- ✓ Rice vinegar.
- ✓ 1 tsp. sesame oil.
- ✓ 1 jar Traeger mandarin glaze.
- ✓ 3/2 tbsp. soy sauce.
- ✓ 2 tbsp. cilantro, finely chopped.
- ✓ To taste cracked black pepper.
- ✓ 1 pinch Jacobsen salt or pure kosher sea salt.
- ✓ 1 whole salmon, cut into fillets.

Preparation:

1. To prepare the marinade for the salmon fillets, you will need to take the Traeger mandarin glaze, rice vinegar, lime juice, soy sauce, cilantro, salt, and pepper in a small bowl and mix it until well combined. Place the cut salmon fillets in the marinade and cover them

with plastic wrap. Place the salmon fillet in the refrigerator for at least an hour.

2. When the salmon fillets are ready, it is time to prepare them. Heat up your grill, preheating it to 350° F.

3. Clear the grates and spray them with cooking spray. Place the salmon fillets directly over the grill grates and turn on the salmon. Cook for about 6 minutes until the top is slightly charred. Carefully flip the salmon pieces with a spatula and cook for another 4 minutes.

4. Remove from heat and serve. Garnish with fresh cilantro and grate some extra lime zest over the top if desired. I like to serve mine along with some cauli rice.

Nutrition:

- Calories: 114.

- Protein: 4.7 g.

- Fat: 5.63 g.

- Carbohydrates: 12.86 g.

- Calcium: 55 mg.

- Magnesium: 23 mg.

- Phosphorus: 83 mg.

- Iron: 0.58 mg.

89. Baked Salmon Cakes

Preparation time: 20 minutes.

Cooking time: 20 minutes.

Servings: 4

Ingredients:

- ✓ 2-lbs. salmon.
- ✓ Salt.
- ✓ Ground black pepper.
- ✓ 1/2 small onion, diced.
- ✓ 1 celery.
- ✓ 1 bell pepper, red.
- ✓ 1 tbsp. dill.
- ✓ 1 tsp. lemon zest.
- ✓ 1/2 tsp. black pepper.
- ✓ 1/4 tsp. coarse sea salt.
- ✓ 1 1/2 tbsp. breadcrumbs.
- ✓ 2 large eggs.
- ✓ 3 tbsp. extra-virgin olive oil.

Preparation:

1. Preheat oven to 400° F. Soak bread in 2 tbsp. water to prepare it for adding to the recipe.

2. Grate the salmon using the large grater, making sure that there are no bones in it.

3. Add diced onions, peppers, and celery.

4. Mix all the ingredients.

5. Add the salmon mixture to the soaked and squeezed breadcrumbs.

6. Form salmon mixture into small patties.

7. In a 13x9 baking dish, add the oil and place the salmon cakes onto the oil.

8. Bake for 20 minutes at 400° F or until salmon is done.

9. Allow resting before serving.

Nutrition:

- Calories: 426.

- Protein: 48.64 g.

- Fat: 23.3 g.

- Carbohydrates: 2.73 g.

- Calcium: 491 mg.

- Magnesium: 75 mg.

- Phosphorus: 772 mg.

- Iron: 1.91 mg.

90. Jerk Shrimp

Preparation time: 15 minutes.

Cooking time: 6 minutes.

Servings: 12

Ingredients:

- ✓ 2 lbs. shrimp, peeled, deveined.
- ✓ 3 tbsp. olive oil.

For the spice mix:

- ✓ 1 tsp. garlic powder.
- ✓ 1 tsp. sea salt.
- ✓ 1/4 tsp. ground cayenne.
- ✓ 1 tbsp. brown sugar.

✓ 1/8 tsp. smoked paprika.

✓ 1 tbsp. smoked paprika.

✓ 1 lime, zested.

Preparation:

1. Switch on the Traeger grill, fill the grill hopper with flavored wood pellets, power the grill on by using the control panel, select smoke on the temperature dial, or set the temperature to 450° F and let it preheat for a minimum of 5 minutes.

2. Meanwhile, prepare the spice mix and for this, take a small bowl, place all of its ingredients in it and stir until mixed.

3. Take a large bowl, place shrimps in it, sprinkle with prepared spice mix, drizzle with oil and toss until well coated.

4. When the grill has preheated, open the lid, place shrimps on the grill grate, shut the grill, and smoke for 3 minutes per side until firm and thoroughly cooked.

5. When done, transfer shrimps to a dish and then serve.

Nutrition:

- Calories: 131.

- Fat: 4.3 g.

91. Grilled Rainbow Trout

Preparation time: 1 hour.

Cooking time: 2 hours.

Servings: 6

Ingredients:

✓ 6 rainbow trout, cleaned, butterfly.

For the brine:

✓ 1/4 cup salt.

✓ 1 tbsp. ground black pepper.

✓ 1/2 cup brown sugar.

✓ 2 tbsp. soy sauce.

✓ 16 cups water.

Preparation:

1. Prepare the brine and for this, take a large container, add all of its ingredients in it, stir until sugar has dissolved, then add trout and let soak for 1 hour in the refrigerator.

2. When ready to cook, switch on the Traeger grill, fill the grill hopper with oak flavored wood pellets, power the grill on by using the control panel, select "smoke" on the temperature dial, or set the temperature to 225° F and let it preheat for a minimum of 15 minutes.

3. Meanwhile, remove trout from the brine and pat dry with paper towels.

4. When the grill has preheated, open the lid, place trout on the grill grate, shut the grill, and smoke for 2 hours until thoroughly cooked and tender.

5. When done, transfer trout to a dish and then serve.

Nutrition:

- Calories: 250.

- Fat: 12 g.

- Carbohydrates: 1.4 g.

- Protein: 33 g.

- Fiber: 0.3 g.

VEGETABLE RECIPES

92. Grilled Zucchini Squash Spears

Preparation time: 5 minutes.

Cooking time: 10 minutes

Servings: 5

Ingredients:

- ✓ 4 zucchinis, cleaned, and ends cut.
- ✓ 2 tbsp. olive oil.
- ✓ 1 tbsp. sherry vinegar.
- ✓ 2 thyme leaves pulled.
- ✓ Salt and pepper to taste.

Intolerances:

- ✓ Gluten-free.
- ✓ Egg-free.
- ✓ Lactose-free.

Preparation:

1. Cut the zucchini into halves then cut each half thirds.

2. Add the rest of the ingredients in a zip lock bag with the zucchini pieces. Toss to mix well.

3. Preheat the wood pellet temperature to 350° F with the lid closed for 15 minutes.

4. Remove the zucchini from the bag and place them on the grill grate with the cut side down.

5. Cook for 4 minutes until the zucchini are tender

6. Remove from grill and serve with thyme leaves. Enjoy.

Nutrition:

- Calories: 74.
- Fat: 5.4 g.
- Carbs: 6.1 g.
- Protein: 2.6 g.

93. Whole Roasted Cauliflower With Garlic Parmesan Butter

Preparation time: 15 minutes.

Cooking time: 45 minutes.

Servings: 5

Ingredients:

- ✓ 1/4 cup olive oil.
- ✓ Salt and pepper to taste.
- ✓ 1 cauliflower, fresh.
- ✓ 1/2 cup butter, melted.
- ✓ 1/4 cup parmesan cheese, grated.
- ✓ 2 garlic cloves, minced.
- ✓ 1/2 tbsp. parsley, chopped.

Intolerances:

- ✓ Gluten-free.
- ✓ Egg-free.

Preparation:

1. Preheat the wood pellet grill with the lid closed for 15 minutes.

2. Brush the cauliflower with oil then season with salt and pepper.

3. Place the cauliflower in a cast iron and place it on a grill grate.

4. Cook for 45 minutes or until the cauliflower is golden brown and tender

5. Mix butter, cheese, garlic, and parsley in a mixing bowl.

6. In the last 20 minutes of cooking, add the butter mixture.

7. Remove the cauliflower and top with more cheese and parsley if you desire. Enjoy.

Nutrition:

- Calories: 156.
- Fat: 11.1 g.
- Carbs: 8.8 g.
- Protein: 8.2 g.

94. Grilled Asparagus and Honey Glazed Carrots

Preparation time: 15 minutes.

Cooking time: 35 minutes.

Servings: 5

Ingredients:

- ✓ 1 bunch asparagus, trimmed ends.
- ✓ 1 lb. carrots, peeled.
- ✓ 2 tbsp. olive oil.
- ✓ Sea salt to taste.
- ✓ 2 tbsp. honey.
- ✓ Lemon zest.

Intolerances:

- ✓ Gluten-free.
- ✓ Egg-free.
- ✓ Lactose-free.

Preparation:

1. Sprinkle the asparagus with oil and sea salt. Drizzle the carrots with honey and salt.

2. Preheat the wood pellet to 165° F with the lid closed for 15 minutes.

3. Place the carrots in the wood pellet and cook for 15 minutes. Add asparagus and cook for 20 more minutes or until cooked.

4. Top the carrots and asparagus with lemon zest. Enjoy.

Nutrition:

- Calories: 1680.

- Fat: 30 g.

- Carbs: 10 g.

- Protein: 4 g.

95. Grilled Vegetables

Preparation time: 5 minutes.

Cooking time: 15 minutes.

Servings: 8

Ingredients:

- ✓ 1 veggie tray.
- ✓ 1/4 cup vegetable oil.
- ✓ 2 tbsp. veggie seasoning.

Intolerances:

- ✓ Gluten-free.
- ✓ Egg-free.
- ✓ Lactose-free.

Preparation:

1. Preheat the wood pellet grill to 375° F.
2. Toss the vegetables in oil then place on a sheet pan.
3. Sprinkle with veggie seasoning then place on the hot grill.

4. Grill for 15 minutes or until the veggies are cooked.

5. Let rest then serve. Enjoy.

Nutrition:

- Calories: 44.

- Fat: 5 g.

- Carbs: 1 g.

- Potassium: 10 mg.

96. Smoked Acorn Squash

Preparation time: 10 minutes.

Cooking time: 2 hours.

Servings: 6

Ingredients:

- ✓ 3 tbsp. olive oil.
- ✓ 3 acorn squash, halved and seeded.
- ✓ 1/4 cup unsalted butter.
- ✓ 1/4 cup brown sugar.
- ✓ 1 tbsp. cinnamon, ground.
- ✓ 1 tbsp. chili powder.
- ✓ 1 tbsp. nutmeg, ground.

Intolerances:

- ✓ Gluten-free.
- ✓ Egg-free.

Preparation:

1. Brush olive oil on the acorn squash cut sides then cover the halves with foil. Poke holes on the foil to allow steam and smoke through.

2. Fire up the wood pellet to 225° F and smoke the squash for 1 ½-2 hour.

3. Remove the squash from the smoker and allow it to sit.

4. Melt butter, sugar, and spices in a saucepan. Stir well to combine.

5. Remove the foil from the squash and spoon the butter mixture in each squash half. Enjoy.

Nutrition:

- Calories: 149.
- Fat: 10 g.
- Carbs: 14 g.
- Protein: 2 g.

97. Vegan Smoked Carrot Hot Dogs

Preparation time: 25 minutes.

Cooking time: 35 minutes.

Servings: 4

Ingredients:

- ✓ 4 thick carrots.
- ✓ 2 tbsp. avocado oil.
- ✓ 1 tbsp. liquid smoke.
- ✓ 1/2 tbsp. garlic powder.
- ✓ Salt and pepper to taste.

Intolerances:

- ✓ Gluten-free.
- ✓ Egg-free.
- ✓ Lactose-free.

Preparation:

1. Preheat the wood pellet grill to 425° F and line a baking sheet with parchment paper.

2. Peel the carrots and round the edges.

3. In a mixing bowl, mix oil, liquid smoke, garlic, salt, and pepper. Place the carrots on the baking dish then pour the mixture over.

4. Roll the carrots to coat evenly with the mixture and use fingertips to massage the mixture into the carrots.

5. Place in the grill and grill for 35 minutes or until the carrots are fork-tender, ensuring to turn and brush the carrots every 5 minutes with the marinade.

6. Remove from the grill and place the carrots in a hot dog bun. Serve with your favorite toppings and enjoy.

Nutrition:

- Calories: 149.
- Fat: 1.6 g.
- Carbs: 27.9 g.
- Protein: 5.4 g.

98. Grilled Spicy Sweet Potatoes

Preparation time: 10 minutes.

Cooking time: 35 minutes.

Servings: 6

Ingredients:

- ✓ 2 lb. sweet potatoes, cut into chunks.
- ✓ 1 red onion, chopped.
- ✓ 2 tbsp. oil.
- ✓ 2 tbsp. orange juice.
- ✓ 1 tbsp. roasted cinnamon.
- ✓ 1 tbsp. salt.
- ✓ 1/4 tbsp. chipotle chili pepper.

Intolerances:

- Gluten-free.
- Egg-free.
- Lactose-free.

Preparation:

1. Preheat the wood pellet grill to 425° F with the lid closed.

2. Toss the sweet potatoes with onion, oil, and juice.

3. In a mixing bowl, mix cinnamon, salt, and pepper then sprinkle the mixture over the sweet potatoes.

4. Spread the potatoes on a lined baking dish in a single layer.

5. Place the baking dish in the grill and grill for 30 minutes or until the sweet potatoes are tender.

6. Serve and enjoy.

Nutrition:

- Calories: 145.
- Fat: 5 g.
- Carbs: 23 g.
- Protein: 2 g.

99. Grilled Mexican Street Corn

Preparation time: 5 minutes.

Cooking time: 25 minutes.

Servings: 6

Ingredients:

- ✓ 6 ears of corn on the cob.
- ✓ 1 tbsp. olive oil.
- ✓ Kosher salt and pepper to taste.
- ✓ 1/4 cup mayo.
- ✓ 1/4 cup sour cream.
- ✓ 1 tbsp. garlic paste.
- ✓ 1/2 tbsp. chili powder.
- ✓ Pinch of ground red pepper.
- ✓ 1/2 cup coria cheese, crumbled.
- ✓ 1/4 cup cilantro, chopped.
- ✓ 6 lime wedges.

Intolerances:

- ✓ Gluten-free.
- ✓ Egg-free.

Preparation:

1. Brush the corn with oil.

2. Sprinkle with salt.

3. Place the corn on a wood pellet grill set at 350° F. Cook for 25 minutes as you turn it occasionally.

4. Mix mayo, cream, garlic, chili, and red pepper until well combined.

5. Let it rest for some minutes then brush with the mayo mixture.

6. Sprinkle cottage cheese, more chili powder, and cilantro. Serve with lime wedges. Enjoy.

Nutrition:

- Calories: 144.

- Fat: 5 g.

- Carbs: 10 g.

VEGAN RECIPES

100. Veggie Burgers

For more heat and a smokier BBQ burger, feel free to replace the ketchup with BBQ sauce and chili sauce and use smoked paprika instead of basil.

Preparation time: 10 minutes.

Cooking time: 20 minutes.

Serving: 4

Ingredients:

- ✓ ¼ cup, quick-cooking rolled oats.
- ✓ 1 cup, textured vegetable protein.
- ✓ ¼ tsp. mustard powder.
- ✓ 2 tbsp. organic ketchup.
- ✓ ¼ cup whole wheat pastry flour.
- ✓ 2 tbsp. soy sauce.
- ✓ 1 tbsp. creamy peanut butter.

- ✓ ¾ cup boiling water.
- ✓ 1 tbsp. nutritional yeast.
- ✓ Dried oregano.
- ✓ ½ tsp. dried basil flakes.
- ✓ ½ tsp. dried parsley flakes.
- ✓ ½ tsp. onion granules.
- ✓ ½ tsp. garlic granules.

267

Preparation:

1. Add the hot water to a large-sized mixing bowl and then add the basil, parsley flakes, mustard powder, oregano, onion, and garlic granules with the textured vegetable protein and oats; mix well.

2. Next, add the organic ketchup and soy sauce to the mixture, let them rest until the textured vegetable protein soaks up the flavors.

3. Add the seed/nut butter and mix them together until nicely incorporated.

4. Add the pastry flour and nutritional yeast and thoroughly mix.

5. Make approximately 4–6 flat patties from the prepared batter using your hands.

6. Over medium heat in a heavy-bottom skillet, add a light coating of high-smoke point oil such as olive oil, grape seed, or canola and cook each patty until turn golden brown on each side, approximately 5–8 minutes.

Nutrition:

- Calories: 1192.

- Fat: 28 g.

- Carbohydrates: 168 g.

- Protein: 68 g.

101. Delicious Fruit Salad

Preparation time: 5 minutes.

Cooking time: 35 minutes.

Servings: 10

Ingredients:

- ✓ 2 medium, diced apples.
- ✓ 1 20 oz. can, drained; reserve the juice pineapple tidbits.
- ✓ 2 medium, diced bananas.
- ✓ 1 box, 1 ½ oz. sugar-free instant vanilla pudding mix.
- ✓ Juice of 1 lemon, freshly squeezed.
- ✓ 2 cups, sliced fresh strawberries.
- ✓ ¼ cup chopped pecans.
- ✓ 2 cups grapes.
- ✓ ½ cup water.

Preparation:

1. Combine apples with lemon juice and bananas in a large-sized and mix them together.

2. Gently toss the ingredients and ensure that the fruit is evenly coated with the lemon juice.

3. After that, add the strawberries, pineapple, pecans, and grapes.

4. Add water followed by pineapple juice and pudding mix in a separate medium-sized mixing bowl and beat until completely smooth.

5. Now, add the smooth pudding mixture over the tossed fruits.

6. Toss them gently for even coating.

7. Freeze them before serving.

Nutrition:

- Calories: 630.

- Fat: 70 g.

- Carbohydrates: 420 g.

- Protein: 170 g.

102. Mashed Potatoes

Preparation time: 5 minutes.

Cooking time: 30 minutes.

Servings: 4

Ingredients:

- ✓ 2 lbs. Yukon gold potatoes, sliced into 2 thick pieces.
- ✓ 1/3 cup extra virgin olive oil.
- ✓ Pepper and salt (to taste).

Preparation:

1. Rinse the potatoes under cold running tap water and then add them to a pot filled with salty water (enough to cover the potatoes).

2. Use a lid, cover the pot, and bring it to a boil over moderate heat, cook for 12–15 minutes, until turn soft and tender.

3. Drain the potatoes well but ensure that you reserve a cup of the cooking liquid. Let the potatoes stay in the strainer.

4. Now, over moderate heat in a large pan, heat up the olive oil until hot, and then remove it from the heat.

5. Push the potatoes from a ricer into the warm oil.

6. Slowly pour in the reserved cooking liquid, if required, and continue to mix.

7. Sprinkle with black pepper and salt to taste.

8. And then, serve and enjoy.

Nutrition:

- Calories: 243 g.
- Fat: 28 g.
- Carbohydrates: 169 g.
- Protein: 69 g.

103. Spicy Poha

Preparation time: 10 minutes.

Cooking time: 20 minutes.

Servings: 4

Ingredients:

- ✓ 3 cups, washed well, and drained thick poha.
- ✓ 1 tsp. black mustard seeds.
- ✓ 5, dried or fresh curry leaves.
- ✓ ½ tsp. turmeric.
- ✓ 1 tsp. cumin seeds.
- ✓ A small pinch of hing.
- ✓ 1 small, finely chopped green chili.
- ✓ ½ cup, chopped fresh cilantro leaves.
- ✓ 1, small, finely chopped onion.
- ✓ 1/3 cup olive oil.
- ✓ Fresh cilantro, coconut, and rice flakes lime, for garnish.
- ✓ ½ tsp. salt.

Preparation:

1. Set your oil to heat on medium heat in a large frying pan. Add the cumin seeds, curry leaves, mustard seeds.

2. Give the ingredients a good stir until the seeds begin to pop and then add the thing followed by turmeric and salt, continue to stir until mixed well.

3. Add the onions, chili, and cilantro, cook slightly brown, and turns soft for a minute or 2 more.

4. Stir in the rice flakes, cover completely and turn off the heat.

5. Let the rice flakes to sit for a few minutes and then garnish with fresh cilantro and coconut flakes. Transfer the cooked poha evenly to 4 large-sized serving plates. Serve immediately and enjoy.

Nutrition:

- Calories: 181.8 g.
- Fat: 1.5 g.
- Carbs: 38.2 g.
- Protein: 9.5 g.

104. Mouthwatering Upma

Preparation time: 5 minutes.

Cooking time: 25 minutes.

Servings: 4

Ingredients:

- ✓ 1 cup creamed wheat.
- ✓ 5 curry leaves.
- ✓ 1 tsp. cumin seeds.
- ✓ ½ tsp. turmeric.
- ✓ 1 small, finely chopped green chili.
- ✓ ¼ cup, chopped fresh cilantro leaves.
- ✓ 1 tsp. black mustard seeds.
- ✓ 3 cups water.
- ✓ 1 small, finely chopped onion.
- ✓ ½ cup olive oil.
- ✓ A small pinch of hing
- ✓ ½ tsp. salt.

For the garnish:

- ✓ Fresh cilantro leaves and coconut flakes.

Preparation:

1. Over medium heat in a large, heavy dry pan, roast the creamed wheat for a few minutes, until it begins to brown slightly, shake or stir frequently to prevent burning, set aside at room temperature until ready to use.

2. After that, over medium heat in a large saucepan, heat the oil until it turns hot then, add the cumin and mustard seeds.

3. Cook until the seeds start to pop and then add the leftover spices (except salt).

4. Stir in the chili, onion, and cilantro then, continue to cook for a couple of more minutes until the onion turns brown.

5. Add the water and salt, bring everything together to a boil.

6. Slowly stir in the roasted mush and let boil for a minute or 2 more, stirring continuously.

7. Garnish with chopped cilantro leaves and coconut flakes.

8. Transfer the cooked upma evenly among 4 plates and squeeze fresh lime over each serving. Serve immediately and enjoy.

Nutrition:

- Calories: 184.8 g.
- Fat: 1.5 g.
- Carbs: 37.2 g.
- Protein: 10.5 g.

105. Blueberry Oatmeal Waffles

Preparation time: 10 minutes.

Cooking time: 55 minutes.

Ingredients:

- ✓ 1 cup quick-cooking oats.
- ✓ 1 ½ cups frozen blueberries.
- ✓ 1/3 cup unsweetened applesauce.
- ✓ 1 cup white whole wheat flour.
- ✓ ¼ tsp. ground allspice.
- ✓ 1 tbsp. baking powder.
- ✓ 1 ½ cups unsweetened almond milk.
- ✓ 3 tbsp. pure maple syrup.
- ✓ 1 tsp. pure vanilla extract.
- ✓ 2 tbsp. canola oil.
- ✓ ½ tsp. salt.

Preparation:

1. Sift the flour with baking powder, allspice, and salt in a large-sized mixing bowl.

2. Add oats and mix well. Make a well in the center and add the applesauce followed by maple syrup, milk,

vanilla, and oil. Give the ingredients a good stir until combined well.

3. Set the batter aside and let rest until it thickens a bit for a few minutes, then fold in the frozen blueberries.

4. Lightly coat standard-sized waffle iron with some oil. Put approximately ½ cup of the prepared batter in each of the waffles and cook per the directions provided by the manufacturer.

Nutrition:

- Calories: 181.8 g.
- Fat: 1.5 g.
- Carbs: 35.2 g.
- Protein: 7.5 g.

106. Carrot Rice With Peanuts

Preparation time: 50 minutes.

Servings: 4

Ingredients:

- ✓ 1 cup basmati.
- ✓ 2 cups water.
- ✓ 1 tbsp. almond butter.
- ✓ ¼ roasted peanuts.
- ✓ 1 tsp. minced gingerroot.
- ✓ ¾ cup grated carrot.
- ✓ Pepper and salt to taste.
- ✓ 1 thinly sliced onion.
- ✓ Fresh cilantro, to garnish

Preparation:

1. Over high heat in a medium-sized saucepan, combine rice with water, then give it a good stir and bring it to a boil.

2. Once done, decrease the heat to low, cover the pan with a lid and let steam until tender and cooked for 15–20 minutes.

3. In the meantime, add peanuts in a blender and pulverize on high power; set aside.

4. Over medium to high heat in a large skillet, heat the butter until melted and sauté the onions for a few minutes until the onions turn golden brown.

5. Add the carrots, ginger, and salt to taste; stir well.

6. Decrease the heat to low, cover, and let steam for 5 minutes.

7. Add in peanuts and pepper; stir well.

8. Add rice, when done to the skillet and gently stir to combine with the leftover ingredients.

9. Just before serving, don't forget to garnish it with freshly chopped cilantro; serve warm and enjoy.

Nutrition:

- Calories: 176.8 g.
- Fat: 1.3 g.
- Carbs: 38.2 g.
- Protein: 9.7 g.

107. Red Chard Saag

Preparation time: 10 minutes.

Cooking time: 40 minutes.

Servings: 6

Ingredients:

- ✓ 2 tbsp. vindaloo curry paste.

- ✓ Basmati rice or Naan bread.

- ✓ 1 bunch, stems removed finely chopped red Swiss chard.

- ✓ 8 tbsp. vegetable oil.

- ✓ 2 medium minced onions.

- ✓ 2 minced garlic cloves.

- ✓ A piece of ginger, preferably 2, minced.

- ✓ ½ cup water.

Preparation:

1. Over medium to high heat in a heavy-bottomed sauté pan, heat the oil until it hot, and then carefully add the onions.

2. Sauté for a minute or 2 until the onions turn transparent.

3. Add in the chopped chard and cook until the chard completely wilt.

4. Add vindaloo, and then decrease the heat.

5. Cover and let simmer until you get your desired consistency, for 15–20 minutes, stirring occasionally.

6. If the mixture is getting dry, feel free to add more water, as required.

7. Increase the heat and then add in the ginger and garlic; stir well.

8. Heat for 5 more minutes.

9. Serve with basmati rice and/or Naan bread.

Nutrition:

- Calories: 179.8 g.

- Fat: 1.8 g.

- Carbs: 33.2 g.

- Protein: 10.5 g.

108. Garlic Pita Naan

Preparation time: 10 minutes.

Cooking time: 20 minutes.

Servings: 6

Ingredients:

- ✓ 8 mini pita pockets.
- ✓ 1–2 peeled and chopped garlic cloves
- ✓ 2 tbsp. chopped fresh parsley.
- ✓ ¼ cup olive oil.
- ✓ 1–2 dashes salt.

Preparation:

1. Preheat your broiler in advance.

2. Combine garlic clove with olive oil, chopped parsley, and salt in a medium-sized mixing bowl, mix them together.

3. Arrange the pitas over a large-sized baking sheet and drizzle a tsp. of the oil-garlic mixture on top.

4. Use the back of a spoon, spread the mixture to the edges of each pita.

5. Broil until turn lightly brown, for a few minutes, ensure that you don't burn them.

6. Enjoy with your favorite hummus.

Nutrition:

- Calories: 179.8 g.
- Fat: 0.8 g.
- Carbohydrates: 34.2 g.
- Protein: 8.6 g.

109. Spiced Sweet Potato Wedges

Preparation time: 5 minutes.

Cooking time: 50 minutes

Servings: 4

Ingredients:

- ✓ 1 tsp. packed brown sugar.
- ✓ 20 oz sweet potatoes scrubbed, cutting each lengthwise into 8 wedges.
- ✓ 1 tbsp. olive oil.
- ✓ ¼ tsp. pumpkin pie spice.
- ✓ ¼ tsp. hot chili powder.
- ✓ ¼ tsp. black pepper.
- ✓ ¼ tsp. smoked paprika.
- ✓ ¼ tsp. kosher salt.

Preparation:

1. Preheat a large-sized baking sheet in your oven at 425° F.

2. Add the sweet potato wedges in a large-sized mixing bowl and then drizzle with some of the olive oil; toss to coat.

3. Next, in a separate small-sized bowl, add the brown sugar followed by the pepper, chili powder, kosher salt, smoked paprika, and pumpkin pie spice, give the ingredients a good stir until they combined well.

4. Sprinkle the spice mixture over the sweet potatoes, give everything a good toss until nicely coated.

5. Arrange the wedges over the prepared baking sheet, preferably in a single layer.

6. Roast until turn browned and fork-tender, for 25–30 minutes, turning the wedges once halfway during the cooking time.

Nutrition:

- Calories: 178.8.

- Fat: 1.8 g.

- Carbohydrates: 33.2 g.

- Protein: 9.0 g.

110. Cheesy Broccoli Pasta

Preparation time: 5 minutes.

Cooking time: 40 minutes.

Servings: 5

Ingredients:

- ✓ 2 cups dried whole-wheat pasta.

- ✓ ½ tsp. onion powder.

- ✓ 4 tbsp. nutritional yeast flakes.

- ✓ ½ head broccoli, cut into small florets.

- ✓ 2 tbsp. plain flour.

- ✓ 1 tsp. dried chives.

- ✓ ½ tsp. Dijon mustard.

- ✓ 1 ½ tbsp. lemon juice, freshly squeezed.

- ✓ 1/8 tsp. black pepper.

- ✓ Dairy-free vegan butter

- ✓ 2 ½–3 cups water.

- ✓ 1 tsp. garlic powder.

- ✓ ¼ tsp. salt.

Preparation:

1. Put the entire ingredients together in the saucepan (except broccoli and the nutritional yeast), give the ingredients a good stir until nicely mixed.

2. Cover the pan with a lid, bring it to a boil over moderate heat, and cook until al dente for 8–10 minutes. During the cooking process, don't forget to stir the contents frequently, and feel free to add more water, if required.

3. After 5 minutes of cooking time, add broccoli florets to the hot pan.

4. After 10 minutes, remove the pan from heat and stir in the nutritional yeast. Let rest for a few minutes. Serve warm and enjoy.

Nutrition:

- Calories: 153.8.
- Fat: 1.5 g.
- Carbs: 40.2 g.
- Protein: 9.5 g.

BAKED RECIPES

111. Low Carb Almond Flour Bread

Preparation time: 10 minutes.

Cooking time: 1 hour 15 minutes.

Servings: 24 slices.

Ingredients:

- ✓ 1 tsp. sea salt or to taste.
- ✓ 1 tbsp. apple cider vinegar.
- ✓ ½ cup warm water.
- ✓ ¼ cup coconut oil.
- ✓ 4 large eggs (beaten).
- ✓ 1 tbsp. gluten-free baking powder.
- ✓ 2 cup blanched almond flour.
- ✓ ¼ cup Phylum husk powder.
- ✓ 1 tsp. ginger (optional).

Preparation:

1. Preheat the grill to 350° F with the lid closed for 15 minutes.

2. Line a 9 by 5-inch loaf pan with parchment paper. Set aside.

3. Combine the ginger, Phylum husk powder, almond flour, salt, baking powder in a large mixing bowl.

4. In another mixing bowl, mix the coconut oil, apple cider vinegar, eggs, and warm water. Mix thoroughly.

5. Gradually pour the flour mixture into the egg mixture, stirring as you pour. Stir until it forms a smooth batter.

6. Fill the lined loaf pan with the batter and cover the batter with aluminum foil.

7. Place the loaf pan directly on the grill and bake for about 1 hour or until a toothpick or knife inserted in the middle of the bread comes out clean.

Nutrition:

- Calories: 93.
- Fat: 7.5 g.
- Cholesterol: 31 mg.
- Sodium: 139 mg.
- Carbohydrate: 3.6 g.
- Fiber: 2.2 g.
- Sugar: 0.1 g.
- Protein: 3.1 g.
- Vitamin D: 3 mcg.
- Calcium: 92 mg.
- Iron: 0 mg.
- Potassium: 13 mg.

112. Breadstick

Preparation time: 10 minutes.

Cooking time: 12 minutes.

Servings: 30 breadsticks.

Ingredients:

- ✓ 1 ½ cup sunflower seeds.
- ✓ ½ tsp. sea salt.
- ✓ 1 egg.
- ✓ 1 tsp. fresh rosemary (finely chopped).
- ✓ 2 tsp. xanthan gum.
- ✓ 2 tbsp. cream cheese.
- ✓ 2 cups grated mozzarella.

Preparation:

1. Preheat the grill to 400° F with the lid closed for 15 minutes.

2. Toss the sunflower seeds into a powerful blender and blend until it smooth and flour-like.

3. Transfer the sunflower seed flour into a mixing bowl and add the rosemary and xanthan gum. Mix and set aside.

4. Melt the cheese in a microwave. To do this, combine the cream cheese and mozzarella cheese in a microwave-safe dish.

5. Place the microwave-safe dish in the grill and heat the cheese on high for 1 minute.

6. Bring out the dish and stir. Place the dish in the grill and heat for 30 seconds. Bring out the dish and stir until smooth.

7. Pour the melted cheese into a large mixing bowl.

8. Add the sunflower flour mixture to the melted cheese and stir the ingredients are well combined.

9. Add the salt and egg and mix thoroughly to form a smooth dough.

10. Measure out equal pieces of the dough and roll into sticks.

11. Grease a baking sheet with oil and arrange the breadsticks into the baking sheet in a single layer.

12. Use the back of a knife or metal spoon to make lines on the breadsticks.

13. Place the baking sheet on the grill and make for about 12 minutes or until the breadsticks turn golden brown.

14. Remove the baking sheet from the grill and let the breadsticks cool for a few minutes.

15. Serve.

Nutrition:

- Calories: 23.
- Fat: 1.9 g.
- Cholesterol: 7 mg.
- Sodium: 47 mg.
- Carbohydrates: 0.6 g.
- Fiber: 0.2 g.
- Protein: 1.2 g.
- Vitamin D: 1 mcg.
- Calcium: 5 mg.
- Iron: 0mg.
- Potassium: 18 mg.

113. Shortbread

Preparation time: 20 minutes.

Cooking time: 20 minutes.

Servings: 16

Ingredients:

- ✓ 2 tsp. cinnamon.
- ✓ ½ cup unsalted butter (softened).
- ✓ 1 large egg (beaten).
- ✓ ½ tsp. salt or to taste.
- ✓ 2 cups almond flour.
- ✓ ¼ cup sugar.
- ✓ 1 tsp. ginger (optional).

Preparation:

1. Preheat the grill to 300° F with the lid closed for 5 minutes.

2. Grease a cookie sheet with oil.

3. In a large bowl, combine the cinnamon, almond flour, sugar, ginger, and salt. Mix thoroughly to combine.

4. In another mixing bowl, whisk the egg and softened butter together.

5. Pour the egg mixture into the flour mixture and mix until the mixture forms a smooth batter.

6. Use a tbsp. to measure out equal amounts of the mixture and roll into balls.

7. Arrange the balls into the cookie sheet in a single layer.

8. Now, use the flat bottom of a clean glass cup to press each ball into a flat round cookie. Grease the bottom of the cup before using it to press the balls.

9. Place the cookie sheet on the grill and bake until browned. This will take about 20–25 minutes.

10. Remove the cookie sheet from the grill and let the shortbreads cool for a few minutes.

11. Serve and enjoy.

Nutrition:

- Calories: 152.

- Fat: 12.7 g.

- Cholesterol: 27 mg.

- Sodium: 124 mg.

- Carbohydrates: 6.5 g.

- Fiber: 1.7 g.

- Sugars: 3.2 g.

- Protein: 3.5 g.

- Vitamin D: 5 mcg.

- Calcium: 6 mg.

- Iron: 0 mg.

- Potassium: 9 mg.

114. Classic Banana Bread

Preparation time: 10 minutes.

Cooking time: 1 hour.

Ingredients:

- ✓ 2 cups all-purpose flour.
- ✓ 3/4 tsp. baking soda.
- ✓ 1/2 tsp. salt.
- ✓ 1 cup sugar.
- ✓ 1/4 cup butter, softened.
- ✓ 2 large eggs.
- ✓ 1 1/2 cups mashed ripe banana (about 3 bananas).
- ✓ 1/3 cup plain low-fat yogurt.
- ✓ 1 tsp. vanilla extract cooking spray.

Preparation:

1. Preheat oven to 350° F.

2. Lightly spoon flour into dry measuring cups; level with a knife. Combine the flour, baking soda, and salt, stirring with a whisk.

3. Place sugar and butter in a large bowl, and beat with a mixer at medium speed until well blended (about 1 minute). Add the eggs, 1 at a time, beating well after each addition. Add banana, yogurt, and vanilla; beat

until blended. Add flour mixture; beat at low speed just until moist. Spoon batter into an 8 1/2 x 4 1/2-inch loaf pan coated with cooking spray.

4. Bake at 350° F for 1 hour or until a wooden pick inserted in the center comes out clean. Cool 10 minutes in pan on a wire rack; remove from pan. Cool completely on wire rack.

Nutrition:

- Calories: 169.6.

- Fat: 4.7 g.

- Carbohydrates: 29.5 g.

- Protein: 4.0 g.

115. Bacon Grilled Cheese Sandwich

Preparation time: 10 minutes.

Cooking time: 7–8 minutes.

Ingredients:

- ✓ 1 lb. apple wood smoked bacon slices, cooked.

- ✓ 8 slices Texas toast.

- ✓ 16 slices cheddar cheese.

- ✓ Mayonnaise.

- ✓ Butter.

Preparation:

1. When ready to cook, set the temperature to 350° F and preheat, lid closed for 15 minutes.

2. Spread a little bit of mayonnaise on each piece of bread, place 1 piece of cheddar on a slice then top with a couple of slices of bacon. Add another slice of cheese then top with the other piece of bread. Spread softened butter on the exterior of the top piece of bread.

3. When the grill is hot, place the grilled cheese directly on a cleaned, oiled grill grate buttered side down. Then spread softened butter on the exterior of the top slice.

4. Cook the grilled cheese on the first side for 5–7 minutes until grill marks develop and the cheese has begun to melt. Flip the sandwich and repeat on the other side.

5. Remove from the grill when the cheese is melted and the exterior is lightly toasted. Enjoy!

Nutrition:

- Calories: 342.

- Fat: 36 g.

- Carbohydrates: 60 g.

- Protein: 29 g.

116. Red Velvet Cake Rolls

Preparation time: 10 minutes.

Cooking time: 50 minutes.

Servings: 10

Ingredients:

- ¼ cup powdered sugar.
- 4 eggs, separated.
- ½ cup plus 1/3 cup granulated sugar, divided.
- 1 tsp. vanilla extract.
- 2 tbsp. (1 oz. bottle) red food coloring.
- 2/3 cup all-purpose flour.
- ¼ cup cocoa.
- ½ tsp. baking powder.
- ¼ tsp. baking soda.
- 1/8 tsp. salt.
- Powdered sugar to sprinkle on top.
- 1 cup pecans, finely chopped.
- Cream cheese filling.
- 8 oz. cream cheese.
- 1 cup powdered sugar.
- 6 tbsp. soft butter.
- 1 tsp. vanilla.

Preparation:

1. Heat oven to 375° F. Line a jelly-roll pan with foil; generously grease foil. Sprinkle linen or thin cotton towel with 1/4 cup powdered sugar.

2. Beat egg whites in large bowl until soft peaks form; gradually add 1/2 cup granulated sugar, beating until stiff peaks form. Beat egg yolks and vanilla in medium bowl on medium speed of mixer for about 3 minutes.

3. Gradually add remaining 1/3 cup granulated sugar; continue beating 2 additional minutes. Place red food color in liquid measuring cup; add water to make 1/3 cup. Stir together flour, cocoa, baking powder, baking soda, and salt. Add to egg yolk mixture alternately with colored water, beating on low speed just until batter is smooth.

4. Gradually fold chocolate mixture into beaten egg whites until well blended. Spread batter evenly in the prepared pan.

5. Bake 12–15 minutes or until top springs back when touched lightly in center. Immediately loosen cake from edges of pan; invert onto prepared towel.

6. Carefully peel off foil. Immediately roll cake and towel together starting from narrow end; place on a wire rack to cool completely. Prepare cream cheese filling. Carefully unroll cake; remove towel. Spread filling over cake. Reroll cake without towel. Wrap filled cake with wax paper and wrap again with plastic wrap.

7. Refrigerate with the seam down for at least 1 hour or until you're ready to serve. Just before serving, sprinkle the top with additional powdered sugar. Drizzle with chocolate syrup and garnish with finely chopped pecans.

8. Cover and keep refrigerated.

9. Cream cheese filling: Beat 1 package (8 oz.) softened cream cheese, 1 cup powdered sugar, 6 tbsp. softened butter or margarine and 1 tsp. vanilla extract in small mixer bowl until smooth. Makes 8–10 servings.

Nutrition:

- Carbohydrates: 64.6 g.

- Fiber: 0.5 g.

- Fat: 33.4 g.

- Cholesterol: 63.8 mg.

117. Southern Muscadine Cake

Preparation time: 15 minutes.

Cooking time: 1 hour.

Servings: 10 slices.

Ingredients:

- ✓ 2 ½ cups muscadines.
- ✓ 1 box white cake mix.
- ✓ 1 small box blackberry Jell-O.
- ✓ ¾ cup oil.
- ✓ 4 eggs.
- ✓ 1 ¼ cup powdered sugar.

Preparation:

1. Cook 2 ½ cups muscadines in 1 ½ cups water until hulls are tender (about 15 minutes).

2. Place in a strainer/sieve on top of a bowl. Using a knife, cut a slash in each 1, and then mash to force juice and pulp through, leaving seeds and hulls.

3. Separate hulls from seeds and discard the seed. Set hulls aside.

4. Mix 1 box of a white cake mix, 1 small box blackberry Jell-O, ¾ cup oil, 4 eggs, and the muscadine juice/pulp, reserving 4 tbsp.

5. Beat until fluffy. Fold hulls into the batter and pour into a greased and floured Bundt pan. Bake at 350° F for about 45 minutes until it is done.

6. While baking, stir together powdered sugar with the reserved 4 tbsp. muscadine juice. Heat if necessary, to blend. When the cake is done, poke holes on the top and pour glaze over.

Nutrition:

- Calories: 324.

- Fat: 18.2 g.

- Carbohydrates: 40.8 g.

- Protein: 4.4 g.

Appetizers and Sides Recipes

118. Atomic Buffalo Turds

Jalapeño peppers loaded down with cream cheese and beat with a Lit'l Smokies sausages are lovingly known as Atomic Buffalo Turds (ABTs). Each chomp gets you an ensemble of flavor layers. In case you're not an enthusiast of jalapeños, have confidence that they get milder as you cook them. For a less zesty other option, substitute infant ringer peppers for the jalapeños.

Preparation time: 30–45 minutes.

Cooking time: 1½–2 hours.

Servings: 6–10

Ingredients:

- ✓ 10 medium jalapeño peppers.

- ✓ 8 oz. customary cream cheese at room temperature.

- ✓ ¾ cup destroyed Monterey Jack.

- ✓ Cheddar cheese blend (optional).

- ✓ 1 tsp. smoked paprika.

- ✓ 1 tsp. garlic powder.

- ✓ 1 tsp. cayenne pepper.

- ✓ 1 tsp. red pepper drops (optional).

- ✓ 20 Lit'l Smokies sausages.

- ✓ 10 meagerly sliced bacon strips, cut down the middle.

Preparation:

1. Put your nourishment administration gloves on, if utilizing. Wash and slice the jalapeño peppers the long way. Utilizing a spoon or paring blade, cautiously evacuate the seeds and veins and dispose of them. Place the jalapeños on the top of a vegetable grilling plate and put it in a safe spot.

2. In a little bowl, blend the cream cheese, destroyed cheese, if utilizing, paprika, garlic powder, cayenne pepper, and red pepper pieces until completely consolidated.

3. Fill the emptied jalapeño pepper parts with the cream cheese blend.

4. Place a Lit'l Smokies wiener over each filled jalapeño pepper half.

5. Fold half a slice of meager bacon over each jalapeño pepper half.

6. Utilize a toothpick to tie down the bacon to the frankfurter, making a point not to puncture the pepper. Place the ABTs on a grilling plate or container.

7. On the wood pellet smoker-grill

8. Design your wood pellet smoker-grill for aberrant cooking and preheat to 250° F utilizing hickory pellets or a blend.

9. Smoke the jalapeño peppers at a temperature of 250° F for around 1½–2 hours, until the bacon is cooked and fresh.

10. Expel the ABTs from the grill and let rest for 5 minutes before filling in as an hors d'oeuvre.

Nutrition:

- Calories: 201.

- Fat: 20 g.

- Carb: 4 g.

- Protein: 7.9 g.

119. Smashed Potato Casserole

Your friends and family will be happy with this decadent and juicy side dish, but easy to prepare. The recipe was inspired by "Sliced Potato Fries" posted by Laurence Hill on pelletheads.com. I first utilized Larry's recipe a few years ago with Thanksgiving mashed potatoes. Layer flavor profiles add new dimensions to potato trays. Feel free to modify this recipe here and there as I have done over the years.

Preparation time: around 30–45 minutes.

Cooking time: 45–60 minutes.

Servings: 8

Ingredients:

- ✓ 8–10 bacon slices.
- ✓ Cup (½ stick) salted butter or bacon grease.
- ✓ 1 small red onion, sliced thinly.
- ✓ 1 small green bell pepper, sliced thinly.
- ✓ 1 small red bell pepper, sliced thinly.
- ✓ 1 small yellow bell pepper, sliced thinly.
- ✓ 3 cups mashed potatoes.
- ✓ ¾ cup sour cream.
- ✓ 1½ tsp. Texas barbecue rub.
- ✓ 3 cups shredded sharp cheddar cheese.

✓ Divided 4 cups frozen
hash brown potatoes.

Preparation:

1. In a large skillet, cook the bacon using medium heat until crisp, about 5 minutes on each side. Set the bacon aside.

2. Transfer the rendered bacon grease inside of a glass container.

3. In the same large skillet using medium heat, warm the butter or bacon grease and sauté the red onion and bell peppers until al dente. Set aside.

4. Spray a 9 by 11-inch casserole dish with nonstick cooking spray, and spread the mashed potatoes in the bottom of the dish.

5. Layer the sour cream over the mashed potatoes and season with Texas Barbecue Rub.

6. Layer the sautéed vegetables on top of the potatoes, retaining the butter or bacon grease in the pan.

7. Sprinkle with 1 and a half cups of the sharp cheddar cheese followed by the frozen hash brown potatoes.

8. Spoon the remaining bacon grease or butter from the sautéed vegetables over the hash browns and top with crumbled bacon.

9. Top with the remaining 1 and a half cups of sharp cheddar cheese and cover the casserole dish with a lid or aluminum foil.

313

10. On the wood pellet smoker-grill

11. Configure the wood pellet smoker-grill for non-direct cooking then preheat to 350° F using your pellets of choice.

12. Bake the mashed potato casserole for about 45–60 minutes, until the cheese is bubbling.

13. Let rest for 10 minutes before serving.

Notes:

1. Leftover instant mashed potatoes or mashed potatoes both work wonderfully in this recipe.

2. Utilize fat-free sour cream, extra-virgin olive oil instead of the butter if counting calories, reduced-fat cheese, and use turkey bacon or skip the bacon.

Nutrition:

- Calories: 197.7
- Fat: 17.3 g.
- Carbohydrates: 2.7 g.
- Protein: 7.9 g.

120. Bacon-Wrapped Asparagus

Every spring, for around 8 to twelve weeks, the vegetable stands and grocery stores are full of it. There are so many different methods to enjoy it—deep-frying, sautéing, steaming, baking, and broiling, to name just a few—but my personal favorite method is grilling bacon-wrapped asparagus on my wood pellet smoker-grill.

Preparation time: 15 minutes.

Cooking time: 25–30 minutes.

Serves: 4–6

Ingredients:

- ✓ 1 lb. fresh thick asparagus which is around 15–20 spears.
- ✓ Extra-virgin olive oil.
- ✓ 5 slices thinly sliced bacon.
- ✓ 1 tsp. Pete's Western Rub or salt and pepper.

Preparation:

1. Snap off the woody parts of asparagus and trim so they are all about the same length.

2. Gap the asparagus into groups of 3 lances and spritz with olive oil. Wrap each pack with 1 bit of bacon and

afterward dust with the flavoring or salt and pepper to taste.

3. On the wood pellet smoker-grill

4. Design your wood pellet smoker-grill for circuitous cooking, setting Teflon-covered fiberglass tangles over the meshes (to keep the asparagus from adhering to the grill grates). Preheat to 400° F utilizing any sort of pellets. The grill can be preheated while preparing the asparagus.

5. Grill the bacon-wrapped asparagus for around 25–30 minutes, until the asparagus is delicate and the bacon is cooked and firm.

Nutrition:

- Calories: 109.6.
- Fat: 8 g.
- Carbohydrates: 3.7 g.
- Protein: 6.6 g.

121. Brisket Baked Beans

Brisket baked beans can without much of a stretch be a meal unto itself. It's an extraordinary method to go through smoked meat brisket scraps—that is, in the event that you have any. These beans are an awesome supplement to any meal as a side or fundamental dish, simple and brisk to amass, and wealthy in sweet and fiery flavors.

Preparation time: 20 minutes.

Cooking time: 1½–2 hours.

Servings: 10–12

Ingredients:

- ✓ 2 tbsp. extra-virgin olive oil

- ✓ 1 big yellow onion, diced.

- ✓ 1 medium green ringer pepper, diced.

- ✓ 1 medium red ringer pepper, diced.

- ✓ 2–6 jalapeño peppers, diced.

- ✓ 3 cups cleaved Texas-style brisket flat.

- ✓ 1 (28-oz.) can baked beans, similar to bush's country-style baked beans.

- ✓ 1 (28-oz.) can pork and beans.

- ✓ 1 (14-oz.) can red kidney beans, flushed, and depleted.

- ✓ 1 cup grill sauce, similar to Sweet Baby Ray's Barbecue Sauce.

- ✓ ½ cup pressed dark colored sugar.

- ✓ 3 garlic cloves, slashed.

- ✓ 2 tsp. ground mustard.

- ✓ Tsp. fit salt.

- ✓ Tsp. dark pepper.

Preparation:

1. In a skillet over medium warmth, warm the olive oil and afterward include the diced onion, peppers, and jalapeños. Cook until the onions are translucent, around 8 minutes, blending every so often.

2. In a 4-quart meal dish, blend the hacked brisket, baked beans, pork and beans, kidney beans, cooked onion and peppers, grill sauce, dark colored sugar, garlic, ground mustard, salt, and dark pepper.

3. On the wood pellet smoker-grill

4. Arrange your wood pellet smoker-grill for roundabout cooking and preheat to 325° F utilizing your pellets of decision. Cook the brisket baked beans revealed for 1½–2 hours until the beans are thick and bubbly.

Notes:

1. Change the warmth factor of the beans by expanding the measure of jalapeño peppers and holding the seeds. Pellet choice isn't significant at 325° F since there will be practically nothing, assuming any, smoke. Whenever wanted, preceding preparing the beans, smoke them for 30–1 hour at 180° F to give them a smoky flavor.

Nutrition:

*   Calories: 200.
*   Fat: 2 g.
*   Carb: 35 g.
*   Protein: 9 g.

122. Garlic Parmesan Wedges

Crispy on the outside and quite tender on the inside, these delectable potato wedges will more than satisfy every French fry fan. The perfect appetizer, side dish, or snack to any meal.

Preparation time: 15 minutes.

Cooking time: 30–35 minutes.

Servings: 4

Ingredients:

- ✓ 3 large russet potatoes.
- ✓ 1 cup extra-virgin olive oil.
- ✓ 1½ tsp. salt.
- ✓ ¾ tsp. black pepper.
- ✓ 2 tsp. garlic powder.

- ✓ ¾ cup grated parmesan cheese.
- ✓ 3 tbsp. finely chopped flat-leaf parsley or fresh cilantro (optional).
- ✓ ½ cup ranch dressing or blue cheese per serving, for dipping (optional).

Preparation:

1. Gently scrub the potatoes using cold water using a vegetable brush and allow the potatoes to dry.

2. Cut the potatoes lengthwise into half, then cut those halves into thirds.

3. Wipe away all the moisture that is released when you cut the potatoes using a paper towel. Moisture prevents the wedges from getting crispy.

4. Place the olive oil, salt, pepper, potato wedges, and garlic powder in a large bowl, and toss lightly using your hands, making sure the oil and spices are distributed evenly.

5. Arrange the wedges into a single layer on a nonstick grilling tray/pan/basket (about 15 × 12 inches).

6. On the wood pellet smoker-grill

7. Configure the wood pellet smoker-grill for non-direct cooking and preheat to 425° F using any type of wood pellets.

8. Place the grilling tray inside of your preheated smoker-grill and roast the potato wedges for 15 minutes before turning. Roast the potato wedges for an additional 20 minutes until potatoes are fork-tender on the inside but crispy golden brown on the outside.

9. Sprinkle the potato wedges along with parmesan cheese and garnish with cilantro or parsley, if desired.

Serve with ranch dressing for dipping or blue cheese, if desired.

Nutrition:

- Calories: 194.3.

- Saturated fat: 1.7 g.

- Total fat: 4.9 g.

- Polyunsaturated Fat: 0.4 g.

123. Roasted Vegetables

Accentuate any main dish with these amazing crispy, caramelized roasted fresh vegetables with delicious flavor from garlic, herbs, and olive oil. These colorful vegetables will lighten up any dinner table. It doesn't get any easier than this.

Preparing time: about 20 minutes.

Cooking time: 20–40 minutes

Servings: 4

Ingredients:

- ✓ 1 cup cauliflower florets.

- ✓ 1 cup small mushrooms, halved.

- ✓ 1 medium zucchini, sliced and halved.

- ✓ 1 medium yellow squash, sliced and halved.

- ✓ 1 average-size red bell pepper which is chopped into 1½ to 2-inch pieces.

- ✓ 1 small red onion, chopped into 1½ to 2-inch pieces.

- ✓ 6 oz. small baby carrots.

- ✓ 6 average stemmed asparagus spears, sliced into 1-inch pieces.

- ✓ 1 cup cherry or grape tomatoes.

- ✓ ¼ cup roasted garlic–flavored extra-virgin olive oil.

- ✓ 2 tbsp. balsamic vinegar.
- ✓ 3 garlic cloves, minced.
- ✓ 1 tsp. dried thyme.
- ✓ 1 tsp. dried oregano.
- ✓ 1 tsp. garlic salt.
- ✓ ½ tsp. black pepper.

Preparation:

1. Place the mushrooms, zucchini, cauliflower florets, yellow squash, red bell pepper, red onion, carrots, asparagus, and tomatoes into a large bowl.

2. Add vinegar, garlic, thyme, olive oil, balsamic oregano, garlic salt, and black pepper to the vegetables.

3. Gently toss the vegetables by hand until they are fully coated with olive oil, herbs, and spices.

4. Scatter your seasoned vegetables evenly onto a nonstick grilling tray/pan/basket (about 15 × 12 inches).

5. On the wood pellet smoker-grill

6. Configure the wood pellet smoker-grill for non-direct cooking and preheat to 425° F using any type of wood pellets.

7. Transfer the grilling tray to the inside of the preheated smoker-grill and roast the vegetables for 20–40 minutes, or till the time the vegetables are al dente. Serve immediately.

Nutrition:

- Calories: 162.
- Carbohydrates: 28 g.
- Fiber: 5 g.
- Protein: 3 g.
- Fat: 5 g.
- Sodium: 426 mg.

SAUSAGE

124. Premium Sausage Hash

Preparation time: 30 minutes.

Cooking time: 45 minutes.

Servings: 4

Ingredients:

- ✓ Nonstick cooking spray.

- ✓ 2 finely minced garlic cloves.

- ✓ 1 tsp. basil, dried.

- ✓ 1 tsp. oregano, dried.

- ✓ 1 tsp. onion powder.

- ✓ 1 tsp. salt.

- ✓ 4–6 cooked smoker Italian sausage (sliced).

- ✓ 1 large-sized bell pepper, diced.

- ✓ 1 large onion, diced.

- ✓ 3 potatoes, cut into 1-inch cubes.

- ✓ 3 tbsp. olive oil.

- ✓ French bread for serving.

Preparation:

1. Pre-heat your smoker to 225° F using your desired wood chips.

2. Cover the smoker grill rack with foil and coat with cooking spray.

3. Take a small bowl and add garlic, oregano, basil, onion powder, and season the mix with salt and pepper

4. Take a large bowl and add sausage slices, bell pepper, potatoes, onion, olive oil, and spice mix

5. Mix well and spread the mixture on your foil-covered rack

6. Place the rack in your smoker and smoke for 45 minutes

7. Serve with your French bread

8. Enjoy!

Nutrition:

- Calories: 193.

- Fats: 10 g.

- Carbohydrates: 15 g.

- Fiber: 2 g.

125. Smoked Sausage Roll

This enticing and well- seasoned appetizer is flavorful, highly satiating, and loaded with zesty and cheesy filling to become a crowd-pleaser.

Preparation time: 15 minutes.

Cooking time: 1 hour 15 minutes.

Servings: 5

Ingredients:

- ✓ 2-lb. breakfast sausage.
- ✓ 1 ½ lb. raw smoked bacon.
- ✓ The rub.
- ✓ 3 tbsp. jalapeño sauce.

- ✓ 8-oz. cream cheese.
- ✓ ¼ cup BBQ rub.
- ✓ 2 jalapeños, seeded and chopped finely.
- ✓ ½ cup spicy sauce.

Preparation:

1. Start the grill on smoke for about 5 minutes while keeping the lid open.

2. Preheat the smoker to 275° F or 135° C for 15 minutes while keeping the lid closed.

3. Begin by flattening the breakfast sausages on parchment paper.

4. After that, combine jalapeño, jalapeño sauce, and cream cheese in a mixing bowl until mixed well.

5. Next, spread this mixture over the flattened sausages while leaving a 1 ½-inch border on all sides.

6. Now, roll the sausages into a log and seal it properly on all sides.

7. Then, wrap the bacon slices over the sausage log.

8. Apply the rub throughout the bacon-wrapped sausage loaf.

9. Finally, transfer the loaf to the smoker and cook for 1 hour or until the internal temperature shows 160° F or 71° C.

10. Once the reading shows the mentioned temperature, apply the loaf again with the spicy sauce and smoke further for 10 more minutes.

11. Allow it to rest for 10 minutes and serve.

Tip:

- Pair it with crackers or aged cheddar cubes.

Nutrition:

- Calories: 248.
- Fat: 19.82 g.
- Carbohydrates: 4.08 g.
- Fibers: 0.18 g.
- Protein: 12.8 g.

126. Smoked Sausage Minestrone

The first time you actually make the soup, you will wonder whether all the ingredients will go together. But then, all the ingredients coalesce perfectly to make this quick and easy soup.

Preparation time: 15 minutes.

Cooking time: 4 hours.

Servings: 8

Ingredients:

- ✓ 1 ½ lb. Italian sausage, fresh.
- ✓ 2 tbsp. olive oil.
- ✓ 1 tsp. oregano.

- ✓ 10 cups water.
- ✓ 2 onions, diced finely.
- ✓ 2 bay leaves.
- ✓ 3 celery stalks.

- ✓ 2 cups peas, frozen.
- ✓ 1 can black beans, washed and drained.
- ✓ 28 oz. can tomatoes, crushed.
- ✓ Kosher salt, as needed.
- ✓ Black pepper, as needed.
- ✓ 2 cups corn, frozen.
- ✓ 1 tsp. thyme.
- ✓ 2 cups macaroni pasta.

Preparation:

1. Preheat the smoker at 250° F or 121° C.

2. Start by placing the sausage on the rack of the smoker about half an inch apart.

3. Smoke it for 3 hours or until the internal temperature reaches 165° F or 73° C.

4. Once the sausage is smoked, heat oil in a large skillet over medium-high heat.

5. To this, stir in the celery, sausage, and onion and cook for 4 to 5 minutes or until soft and cooked.

6. Next, spoon in the crushed tomatoes, corn, water, peas, and beans into the skillet and bring the mixture to a boil.

7. Reduce the heat and allow it to simmer.

8. Now, spoon in the salt, herbs, pepper and simmer it for around 15–20 minutes.

9. Check the consistency of the soup and add more water if needed.

10. Serve it hot.

Tip:

- Pair it with roasted buns for a complete meal.

Nutrition:

- Calorie: 336.

- Fat: 10 g.

- Protein: 25 g.

- Fiber: 4 g.

127. Smoked Pepperoni Pizza

Just a few ingredients and a good Italian sausage turn this into a meal that will be relished by everyone. It is brilliantly simple and tempting.

Preparation time: 15 minutes.

Cooking time: 2 hours 45 minutes.

Servings: 4

Ingredients:

✓ 1 lb. Italian sausage meat.

✓ ½ cup pepperoni slices.

✓ ¾ cup mozzarella cheese, grated.

✓ ½ cup green olives, sliced.

✓ ¾ cup pizza sauce.

Preparation:

1. Preheat the smoker to 250° F or 125° C for 15 minutes while keeping the lid closed.

2. To begin with, mix the sausage meat with the olives well.

3. After that, roll the meat into a 10 inch by 10 inch square on parchment paper.

4. Next, place the pepperoni slices in the middle portion of the square.

5. Top it with the cheese and roll up the meat square.

6. Now, arrange the roll onto the smoker and smoke it for 2 ½ hours or until the internal temperature reaches 165° F or 71° C.

7. Serve it along with the pizza sauce.

Tip:

- You can even try adding bacon to the roll.

Nutrition:

- Calories: 285.

- Fat: 10.4 g.

- Sodium: 640 mg.

- Carbohydrates: 35.7 g.

- Fiber: 2.5 g.

- Sugars: 3.8 g.

- Protein: 12.2 g

128. Smoked & Spicy Pepper Sausage

Full of flavor, this smoked and spicy pepper sausage that has a little bit of all flavors is a total crowd-pleaser.

Preparation time: 3 hours.

Cooking time: 4 hours.

Servings: 8

Ingredients:

- ✓ 2-lb. beef, grounded.
- ✓ 3 tbsp. curing salt.
- ✓ 1 tsp. black peppercorns, whole.
- ✓ 3 tbsp. Worcestershire sauce.
- ✓ 2 tsp. red pepper flakes.
- ✓ 1 tbsp. black pepper, freshly ground.
- ✓ 2 tbsp. honey.
- ✓ 2 tsp. mustard, whole.

For the fire:

- Start the grill on smoke for about 5 minutes while keeping the lid open.
- Preheat the smoker at 150° F or 65° C.

Preparation:

1. For the first step, combine all the ingredients needed to make the sausage excluding honey in a large-sized mixing bowl and make a mixture out of it.

2. Then, place it in the refrigerator for a day to cure.

3. After that, roll them into logs and wrap them with a plastic cover while rolling out all the air pockets.

4. Tie up the ends.

5. After 2 days, take the meat logs out and apply the honey lightly over them.

6. Finally, place the rolls onto the smoker and smoke it for 3–4 hours or until it reaches an internal temperature of 170° F or 75 ° C.

7. Serve hot.

Tip:

- You can leave the roll in the smoke setting depending on how smoky you want.

Nutrition:

- Calorie: 250.
- Fat: 20 g.
- Protein: 17 g.

129. Smoked Bacon & Sausage Bomb

This is quite simply the best-smoked meatloaf ever. With Italian sausages, smoking raw bacon, 2 types of cheese, jalapeño, BBQ sauce, and garlic in it, this fare creates an explosion of flavor for your taste buds the moment you take your first bite.

Preparation time: 15 minutes.

Cooking time: 3 hours 40 minutes.

Servings: 8

Ingredients:

✓ 2-lb. smoking raw bacon, thick-cut, and divided.

✓ 3 ½ oz. Italian sausage.

The rub:

- ✓ 1 cup cheddar and Monterey jack cheese, shredded finely.

- ✓ 4 garlic cloves, finely minced.

- ✓ ¼ cup jalapeño, finely diced.

- ✓ ¼ cup barbeque seasoning.

- ✓ 2 green onions, finely sliced.

- ✓ 18 oz. can barbeque sauce.

Preparation:

1. Prepare the charcoal smoker about half an hour before it starts cooking.

2. Begin by weaving ¾ portion of the bacon slices in a lattice and then sprinkle the barbeque seasoning over the bacon.

3. After that, heat a non-stick skillet over medium-high heat and cook the remaining bacon for about 8 to 10 minutes until it is crispy.

4. Next, place the sausage in a Ziploc bag and seal it.

5. Now, flatten the sausages into flat shapes and place the sausages over the bacon slices in the lattice.

6. Then, crumble the cooked bacon pieces and spoon them over the sausage pieces.

7. Add the cheese blend, green onions, garlic, and jalapeno over it.

8. On to its top, spoon in the barbeque sauce and barbeque seasoning.

9. Finally, roll the sausages and bacon layers into logs.

10. Arrange the logs with the seam side down over the wired cooking rack.

11. Place the wire racks over the smoker and smoke for about 2 hours or until it is no longer pink in color.

12. During the last half hour of the session, spoon in the barbeque sauce and juice back into it frequently so that it remains moist.

13. The final cooked meat should show an internal temperature reading of 165° F or 75° C at the center.

14. Spoon in remaining barbeque sauce over the sausage roll and allow it to cool for about 15–20 minutes before serving.

Tip:

- Instead of using Italian sausages, you can also breakfast sausages also.

Nutrition:

- Calorie: 608.

- Fat: 42 g.

- Fiber: 0.6 g.

- Protein: 32 g.

130. Breakfast Sausage

Preparation time: 5 minutes.

Cooking time: 30 minutes.

Servings: 6–8

Ingredients:

- 12 breakfast links.

- 1 tbsp. mustard, Dijon-style.

- ½ cup apricot jam.

Preparation:

1. Open the grill and start on Smoke. Once you have a fire, close the lid and let it preheat to 350° F.

2. In a saucepan, warm the apricot jam mixed with the mustard.

3. Place the sausages on the grate and cook for 15 minutes, turning them 2 times. Use tongs and rill the sausages a few times in the sauce mixture and grill for 3 more minutes.

4. Serve with the sauce mixture and enjoy!

Nutrition:

- Calories: 180.

- Proteins: 15 g.

- Carbohydrates: 18 g.

- Fat: 20 g.

131. Spicy Sausage & Cheese Balls

Preparation time: 20 minutes.

Cooking time: 40 minutes.

Servings: 4

Ingredients:

- ✓ 1lb hot breakfast sausage.
- ✓ 2 cups bisquick baking mix.
- ✓ 8 oz. cream cheese.
- ✓ 8 oz. extra sharp cheddar cheese.
- ✓ 1/4 cup Fresno peppers.
- ✓ 1 tbsp. dried parsley.
- ✓ 1 tsp. killer hogs AP rub.
- ✓ 1/2 tsp. onion powder.

Preparation:

1. Get ready smoker or flame broil for roundabout cooking at 400° F.

2. Blend sausage, baking mix, destroyed cheddar, cream cheddar, and remaining fixings in a huge bowl until all-around fused.

3. Utilize a little scoop to parcel blend into chomp to estimate balls and roll tenderly fit as a fiddle.

4. Spot wiener and cheddar balls on a cast-iron container and cook for 15 minutes.

5. Present with your most loved plunging sauces.

Nutrition:

- Calories: 95.

- Carbohydrates: 4 g.

- Fat: 7 g.

- Protein: 5 g.

132. Breakfast Sausage Casserole

Preparation time: 15 minutes.

Cooking time: 30 minutes.

Servings: 6

Ingredients:

- ✓ 1-lb. ground sausage.
- ✓ 1 tsp. ground sage.
- ✓ ¼ cup green beans (chopped).
- ✓ 2 tsp. yellow mustard.
- ✓ 1 tsp. cayenne.
- ✓ 8 tbsp. mayonnaise.

- ✓ 1 large onion (diced).
- ✓ 2 cups diced zucchini.
- ✓ 2 cups shredded cabbage.
- ✓ 1 ½ cup shredded cheddar cheese.
- ✓ Chopped fresh parsley to taste.

Preparation:

1. Preheat the grill to 360° F and grease a cast-iron casserole dish.

2. Heat a large skillet over medium to high heat.

3. Toss the sausage into the skillet, break it apart and cook until browned, stirring constantly.

4. Add the cabbage, zucchini, green beans, and onion and cook until the vegetables are tender, stirring frequently.

5. Pour the cooked sausage and vegetables into the casserole dish and spread it.

6. Break the eggs into a mixing bowl and add the mustard, cayenne, mayonnaise, and sage. Whisk until well combined.

7. Stir in half of the cheddar cheese.

8. Pour the egg mixture over the ingredients in the casserole dish.

9. Sprinkle with the remaining shredded cheese.

10. Place the baking dish on the grill and bake until the top of the casserole turns golden brown.

11. Garnish with chopped fresh parsley.

Nutrition:

- Calories: 472.

- Total fat: 37.6 g.

- Saturated fat: 13.9 g.

- Cholesterol: 98 mg.

- Sodium: 909 mg.

- Total Carbohydrate 10.7 g.

- Dietary Fiber 1.9 g.

133. Smoked Pork Sausages

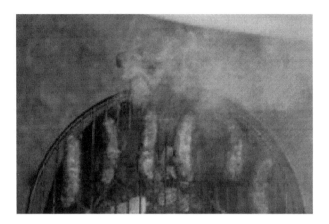

Preparation time: 10 minutes.

Cooking time: 1 hour.

Servings: 6

Ingredients:

- ✓ 3 lbs. ground pork.
- ✓ ½ tbsp. ground mustard.
- ✓ 1 tbsp. onion powder.
- ✓ 1 tbsp. garlic powder.
- ✓ 1 tsp. pink curing salt.
- ✓ 1 tsp. salt.
- ✓ 1 tsp. black pepper.
- ✓ ¼ cup of ice water.
- ✓ Hog casings, soaked and rinsed in cold water.

Preparation:

1. Mix all ingredients except for the hog casings in a bowl. Using your hands, mix until all ingredients are well-combined.

2. Using a sausage stuffer, stuff the hog casings with the pork mixture.

3. Measure 4 inches of the stuffed hog casing and twist to form into a sausage. Repeat the process until you create sausage links.

4. When ready to cook, fire the Traeger grill to 225° F. Use apple wood pellets when cooking the ribs. Close the lid and preheat for 15 minutes.

5. Place the sausage links on the grill grate and cook for 1 hour or until the internal temperature of the sausage reads at 155° F.

6. Allow resting before slicing.

Nutrition:

- Calories: 688.

- Protein: 58.9 g.

- Carbohydrates: 2.7 g.

- Fat: 47.3 g.

- Sugar: 0.2 g.

DESSERT

134. Apple Pie Packet

Preparation time: 5 minutes.

Cooking time: 15 minutes.

Serving: 1

Ingredients:

- ✓ 1 apple.
- ✓ 1 tbsp. butter.
- ✓ 1 1/2 tbsp. brown sugar.
- ✓ 1 tbsp. dried fruit, e.g. B. Raisins.
- ✓ Cinnamon.

Preparation:

1. Preheat the grill.

2. Cut a piece of aluminum foil (approx. 30 x 40 cm). If possible, use film with a non-stick coating, otherwise spray the film on 1 side with non-stick spray before step 3.

3. Place the apple pieces in the middle of the foil, add the butter, brown sugar, cinnamon, and dried fruits.

4. Close the film by folding it. Make sure that the ingredients have some air and that the package is not too tight.

5. Live the packet on the grill and grill for about 15 minutes over medium heat.

6. Carefully, e.g. B. with grill tongs, remove from the grill, place the parcel on a plate. Open carefully as hot steam will escape.

7. Eat apples straight from the packet.

Nutrition:

- Calories: 410.

- Total fat: 19.4 g.

- Carbohydrates: 37.5 g.

- Fiber: 3 g.

135. Apple Pie, From the Pan

Apple pie without a baking tray, easy and quick with just a pan.

Preparation time: 10 minutes.

Cooking time: 40 minutes.

Serving: 8

Ingredients:

- ✓ 250 g. flour.
- ✓ 250 g. apples.
- ✓ 3 eggs.
- ✓ 2 tbsp. cane sugar.
- ✓ 1 dash of lemon.
- ✓ 1 tbsp. baking powder.
- ✓ 150 g. butter.
- ✓ 150 g. cane sugar.
- ✓ 2 tsp. grated orange peel.

Preparation:

1. Cut the apples into pieces, grease the pan.

2. Add lemon juice, sugar, and apple pieces to the pan. Sauté the mixture for a few minutes.

3. Mix the batter in a bowl made of baking powder, flour, eggs, cane sugar, lemon, and orange peel. Then pour this batter over the apples.

356

4. Smooth out the mixture, then close the pan with a lid. Bake on medium heat for 10 minutes. Then set to the lowest setting and continue baking for 10 minutes. It should take about 10–15 minutes for the cake to bake through.

5. Place a cake platter or a large cutting board on the pan. Then turn the pan with the plate.

6. Sprinkle with powdered sugar to taste.

136. Ice Cream

Make ice cream yourself while camping? Only works if you have a fridge in your camper.

Preparation time: 12 hours.

Cooking time: N/A

Servings: 1–10

Ingredients:

- Cream.

- Sugar, to taste.

- Flavors of your choice, e.g. B. strawberry powder.

Preparation:

1. Beat the cream with a whisk.

2. Stir in other ingredients.

3. Let rest in the fridge (freezer) overnight.

Nutrition:

- Calorie: 140.

- Total fat: 7 g.

- Cholesterol: 30 mg.

- Protein: 2 g.

- Total carbohydrates: 17 g.

- Sugar: 14 g.

137. Baked Peach

Preparation time: 2 minutes.

Cooking time: 10 minutes.

Serving: 1

Ingredients:

- ✓ 1/8 cup marshmallows.
- ✓ 1 peach.
- ✓ 1 tbsp. butter.
- ✓ 1 tsp. cinnamon.
- ✓ Garnish, to taste (e.g. berries, peanuts, coconut...).

Preparation:

1. At home: prepare all ingredients in separate bags or containers. Store peaches in such a way that they are not crushed or damaged.

2. On the go: cut the peaches in half, remove the seeds, fill with marshmallows and butter and sprinkle both halves with cinnamon.

3. Wrap the peach halves in aluminum foil and bake over a campfire for 3–5 minutes.

Nutrition:

- Calories: 94.7.
- Sugars: 0.0 g.
- Dietary fiber: 2.0 g.
- Total fat: 2.1 g.

138. Baked Cinnamon Apples

Preparation time: 10 minutes.

Cooking time: 40 minutes.

Servings: 4

Ingredients:

- ✓ 1 apple, medium-sized.
- ✓ 1/2 tsp. cinnamon.
- ✓ 1/2 tsp. sugar.
- ✓ Aluminum foil.

Preparation:

1. Cut the apple on 3 sides from top to bottom, but do not cut through the bottom completely. Core or not to taste.

2. Place the apple on a piece of aluminum foil to later wrap the apple in.

3. Carefully expand the apple incisions, add cinnamon and sugar.

4. Wrap the apple in foil, then close it securely.

5. Bake on the coals of a campfire for about 20–30 minutes.

Nutrition:

- Calories: 214.1.
- Sodium: 55.8 mg.
- Sugars: 52.5 g.
- Protein: 0.4 g.

139. Grilled Pineapple

Preparation time: 5 minutes.

Cooking time: 20 minutes.

Servings: 4

Ingredients:

- ✓ 1 pineapple, cut into long pieces.
- ✓ 1/2 cup of brown sugar.
- ✓ 1/2 cup butter melted.
- ✓ 1 tsp. cinnamon.

Preparation:

1. Place the pineapple pieces in a pan, sprinkle with cinnamon.

2. Mix the cinnamon, butter, and brown sugar together, then spread over the pineapple.

3. Grill for 7–10 minutes, or until the pineapple turns golden brown.

Nutrition:

- Calories: 67.1.
- Total carbohydrates: 17.1 g.
- Sugars: 0.0 g.
- Total fat: 0.4 g.

140. Grilled Fruits

Preparation time: 3 minutes.

Cooking time: 15 minutes.

Servings: 4

Ingredients:

✓ Fruit according to taste and season.

Preparation:

1. Cut the fruit in half, remove the core.

2. Place on a grill with the peel facing up.

3. Grill for about 5 minutes until the fruit is soft and lightly browned.

Nutrition:

- Calories: 171.2.

- Saturated fat: 0.6 g.

- Total fat: 4.0 g.

- Polyunsaturated Fat: 0.5 g.

Manufactured by Amazon.ca
Bolton, ON

25885281R00208